M000203358

Philip Jodidio

tree houses

FAIRY-TALE CASTLES IN THE AIR

Illustrations by
Patrick Hruby

TASCHEN

i also was an arcadian

INTRODUCTION BY PHILIP JODIDIO

The idea of the "tree of life" has run through religion, philosophy, and mythology since the earliest times, from ancient Egypt to China and pre-Columbian Mesoamerica. With its roots in the earth and branches in the sky, the tree is the model of Gothic architecture. Without trees in the forest there would be no columns, and perhaps no temples. Halfway between heaven and earth, the tree has always been impressive for its size, strength, and longevity; a place to dream and a place to find refuge. From vertiginous heights, a man in a tree could look down on daily existence like a bird in flight, a step to breaking the bounds of the ordinary, a hint of immortality.

The fact that in some climates and cultures tree houses are one of the most ancient forms of dwelling is brought home by the continued existence of people such as the Kombai and Korowai, who live in the foothills of the Jayawijaya Mountains in the southwest of Irian Jaya (Indonesia). Apparently pushed upward by pests and tribal rivalries, these people still build houses as much as 40 meters above ground.

If tree houses reach back into the mists of time and are surely one of the earliest forms of architecture, they also populate the history and art of Europe from the times of the Romans. In his *Natural History*, Pliny the Elder wrote of "the Emperor Caligula, who on an estate at Velletri was impressed by the flooring of a single plane tree, and benches laid loosely on beams consisting of its branches, and held a banquet in the tree." It is known that during the Middle Ages monks built small hermitages in trees near monasteries in Europe, but far more spectacular tree houses were imagined in Italy with the Renaissance.

From Caligula to a Dominican Monk

Caligula lived between AD 12 and 41 and, more than 1500 years later, tree houses were still an amusement of the powerful in Italy. At the Villa di Castello in Tuscany, Cosimo I de' Medici (1519–74), the first Duke of Tuscany, had a garden designed by Niccolò Tribolo in 1538 that included a tree house concealed in an ivy-covered oak tree with a square dining room inside the tree. In his book *Treehouses*, Anthony Aikman quotes from Giorgio Vasari's description of this Medici garden: "There were terraces and avenues and orchards, and in a meadow to the east of the villa he planted a holm oak ... so thickly covered with ivy that it looked like a thicket. He constructed a stepped walkway climbing up into it, and at the top a large platform and seats ... with backs all of living green. And in the middle a marble table with a vase of variegated marble into which water is brought by a pipe, which spouts into the air and is carried off by another pipe." The description is by Vasari, who visited Castello often. He adds: "The pipes are so covered with

ivy that they cannot be seen and the water is controlled by taps. It is impossible to describe how the water is carried along the branches of this tree, to sprinkle people and to make fearful hissing sounds." It is quite likely that Tribolo got his idea from reading *Hypnerotomachia Poliphili* written by a Dominican monk, Francesco Colonna. In this poetic story of a journey through an imaginary landscape, the narrator finds himself in an arbor formed by the intertwined branches of fruit trees: "The bowghes were so artificially twisted and growne together that you might ascend up by them and not bee scene in them, nor yet the way where you went up."[1]

The Fountain of Oak

Cosimo I de' Medici's son Francesco de' Medici (1541–87) in turn commissioned a tree house for the Villa di Pratolino (Vaglia, Tuscany, 1569–81), dubbed La Fonte delle Rovere ("The Fountain of Oak"), with spiral staircases leading to a platform set 7.5 meters off the ground. As Aikman explains: "To outdo the tree house at Castello, Francesco encircled the holm oak at Pratolino with not one but two staircases! They spiralled up, parallel to one another on opposite sides of the tree. Stepped ramps rather than staircases, they led high up to where a platform eight meters in diameter had been created among the topmost branches. On this platform were a marble table, seats and fountains that were fed from water piped along the branches."

The French writer Michel de Montaigne (1533–92) wrote of Pratolino after he visited in about 1580.

The English traveler Fynes Moryson (1566–1630) attests to the existence of a tree house with running water in Switzerland (Schaffhausen) in the 1590s, while paintings by Pieter Bruegel and others show Flemish examples in the same period. England, of course, is one of the great countries of the historic tree house with such examples as the early 17th-century structures formed with bent branches at Cobham Hall in Kent, or the surviving example at Pitchford Hall near Shrewsbury in Shropshire, first recorded in 1692. Very early, in the late 18th century, the very European and somewhat patrician fashion for tree houses crossed the Atlantic when the American patriot John Ross built a tree house in the gardens of the Grange Estate in Havertown, Pennsylvania.[2]

Der Schweizerische Robinson Meets Walt Disney

Though some of these historic examples have an almost "legendary" air to them, it might be noted that in the 19th century tree houses entered another phase, one where fact and fiction began to blend. In 1845, a cabaret in the form of interconnected tree houses called *Le grand Robinson* opened in the town of Le Plessis-Piquet near Paris. At its height, this cabaret had as many as 200 tables. The name of the cabaret derived from the 1812 novel *Der Schweizerische Robinson* (Swiss Family Robinson) written by the Swiss pastor Johann David Wyss. The very un-Swiss name Robinson was in fact borrowed from Daniel Defoe's 1712 novel *Robinson Crusoe*. In 1909, Le Plessis-Piquet was renamed Le Plessis-Robinson, an unexpected homage to two books and to a cabaret in a tree house.

The story of the tree house occupied by the *Swiss Family Robinson* has a further and equally surprising twist. Subsequent to a 1960 film made of the book by Walt Disney, the Swiss Family Robinson Tree House has become a fixture in Disney parks throughout the world. Although it is intended to look like the real tree in the movie, this 18-meter-high Disney version is made of steel, concrete, and stucco. With its 1400 branches and 300 000 polyethylene leaves, plus a bit of real Spanish moss, this strange structure stands witness to the popular power of the myth of the tree house. Returning to the earliest ideas of the significance of the tree, Disney's Animal Kingdom theme park includes a "Tree of Life" inspired by the Swiss Family Robinson attraction.

Pretty Julia in the Redwood

The history of the tree houses presented in this book thus extends back in some sense even beyond recorded history. Many of the same ideas that inspired early tree houses are still very much present in their contemporary descendants, from the desire for isolation to the proximity of nature or the vertiginous sensation of being perched high above the ground. The rise of interest in ecologically responsible or sustainable housing and architecture in Europe and the United States in particular, since the 1990s, has certainly contributed to the increase in the number of firms specializing in the design and construction of tree houses. This rise of course mirrors a substantial and sustained surge in public interest in all kinds of tree houses, from simple platforms to elaborate getaways with plasma-screen televisions and intrusion alarms. The living tree is clearly one of the most potent symbols of nature, and its defense, couched occasionally in the rhetoric of radical ecologists, has also been symbolically incarnated by a form of tree house. The American environmentalist Julia "Butterfly" Hill created two three-square-meter platforms 60 meters from the ground in a 1500-year-old California redwood, and spent 738 days there between 1997 and 1999, seeking to prevent loggers from cutting it down. Her act has come to be considered a kind of high point of ecological activism in the United States, and was celebrated in a number of popular songs.

To Relax, to Daydream...

What is new in tree houses in the past 10 or 15 years is the appearance of a number of highly trained and competent designers who have made this area their specialty. One of these is the former cabinet-maker Andreas Wenning, born in 1965 in Germany. Based in Bremen, he has created a number of very contemporary tree houses, some of which are published in this volume. Wenning's introduction to his web site sums up the feeling of excitement and discovery that his work and that of other contemporary tree-house designers elicits: "A tree house! A promise of adventure for the kids, a retreat for the adults, a romantic hideaway close to nature. These special little dwellings installed up

among the trees fire our imagination and arouse our curiosity, bringing back childhood memories, and with them the desire to climb up and enter a magic world amongst the foliage. To be spellbound again, to witness the different sights and sounds up there by day and night and throughout the seasons. To play up there, to work undisturbed, to relax, to daydream..." Wenning's built designs certainly exemplify the application of the principals of design and architecture to the tree-house form, but, even more surprising, his unbuilt work stretches into the domain of cutting-edge forms. For example, his Magnolia and Fir (page 226), Meditation (page 232), and Between Alder and Oak (page 50) tree houses make use of his knowledge of trees, but also become astonishingly "with-it" very much in the spirit of things that are being done in earth-bound buildings. Despite all the gadgetry and modernity introduced in other tree-house designs around the world, Wenning has positioned himself as something of a leader in the domain of contemporary tree-house design.

A Bridge, a Teepee, and a Sailboat

Modern design as it can be adapted to tree-house structures is also the theme chosen by the young American designer Dustin Feider (O2 Treehouse) who makes use of such materials as HDPE (recycled plastic bottles) and the form of Buckminster Fuller's geodesic structures, known to be the most economical in terms of the quantity of materials required for a given volume (page 148). His design for the Blum Tree House (Hollywood, California, USA, 2009) takes on the form of a bridge, while Tree Pi (Santa Monica, California, USA, 2009) works with the equally simple shape of a teepee. Feider, who is in his early 20s, certainly represents a new generation of tree-house builders who have a good knowledge of forms and their dynamics while not being afraid to experiment and to apply the lessons of contemporary architecture to the world of trees. While geodesic structures basically can assume the form of a triangulated sphere in the tree-house context, another North American designer, Tom Chudleigh, has inspired himself from the world of boatbuilding to imagine his Free Spirit Spheres (Qualicum Bay; page 134), suspended in midair on a site in British Columbia, Canada. Even the suspension points of his spheres are related to sailboat design, surely a good example to follow for an object that may well sway with the winds, but an unexpected reference nonetheless.

Fairy-Tale Castles in the Air

In point of fact, many if not most tree-house designers intentionally eschew the image of modernity that Andreas Wenning or Dustin Feider now defend. Their goal is, on the contrary, to perpetuate the "fairy-tale" image that tree houses can easily incarnate. This is the case of the often thatched and shingled structures created by the English firm Blue Forest. Their High-Tech Hideaway (Athens, Greece, 2004) combines a thatched roof with a sophisticated closed-circuit camera system and flat-screen TV. Very much like a comfortable home inside, this structure appears to make a compromise between the presence of modernity and an appearance that relates more readily to Sherwood Forest than to Silicon Valley. The design of Blue Forest for the Treetop Dining Room, (Leatherhead, Surrey, UK) might readily bring to mind the nearly legendary tree houses of England or even those of the Medici. Imagine a splendid dinner in the trees for the famous or less famous. In the trees, any fantasy can come true.

Two French firms take different, but very ambitious, approaches to the world of tree-house design. The first of these, called Dans mon Arbre, is based in Grenoble. Under the direction of Frank Coursier, the firm is very careful to create and execute designs that are respectful of the host trees. Given the different ways the firm designs tree houses, the work of Dans mon Arbre is not necessarily immediately recognizable. Their Langeais design (Langeais Castle Tree House, Parc de l'An Mil, Château de Langeais, France, 2008; page 216) is an assemblage of forms and colors that would not be repudiated by many contemporary architects. Working with designer Renaud Morel, Dans mon Arbre takes several more steps in the direction of work that might readily be classified in the company of earth-bound architecture at quite a high level. Their Kapellerput Tree House (Eindhoven, The Netherlands, 2010; page 196) boasts a total area of 165 square meters, far more than your average tree house. The Aerial Village (2009; page 40), an as yet unbuilt scheme developed with Benoît Fray, is made up of a series of self-supporting, larch-framed, hotel-type accommodations with interior areas of 33 square meters. At the other end of the design spectrum, the Boat Tree House (near Paris, France, 2009) is a €12 000 structure built for children in a maple tree. This tree house does not seek to exist at the cutting edge of architecture, but instead successfully pursues the very laudable goal of making children happy—one of the real purposes of many of the tree houses published in this book.

And Sometimes to Love

The work of La Cabane Perchée, a firm based in the South of France and created in 2000 by Alain Laurens, seeks to provide very sophisticated and intelligent designs while remaining in the aesthetic register of the tree house. Hidden in the leaves, often reached by vertiginous spiraling stairways, these structures, built with the collaboration of master-carpenter Ghislain André, are intended principally for adults "to observe, to read or write, to listen to music, to feel well, to dream, sometimes to be alone, and sometimes to love," as Laurens puts it. Significantly though, Laurens points out that even when tree houses are meant for adults they are often the result of childhood dreams—those of the client, or, of course, those of the designers and builders. This work, usually accompanied by very attractive watercolors painted by Daniel Dufour, has been widely published in books put together by the firm's principals. La Cabane Perchée has built more than 220 tree houses in Europe, often for very prestigious private clients, making it one of the most accomplished companies in this area.

Despite this broad success, La Cabane Perchée, like most tree-house companies, remains very much based in the work of artisans as opposed to a more industrial approach that people like Ghislain André generally eschew. Indeed, each tree house, like each tree, tends to be unique, and that is one reason that this type of "architecture" challenges many of the assumptions of other built forms. Tree houses often require strictly controlled building permits, depending on where they are erected of course, and this simple fact does tend to place them in the domain of architecture, even if many of the designers and builders cited in this volume do not have a degree in engineering or architecture. Carpenters and arborists are probably more present here than architects in the more traditional sense of the profession.

Planting the Tree House Seed

Aside from companies of varying sizes like Blue Forest or La Cabane Perchée, the world of tree-house design and building is populated by a number of strong personalities, for the most part men who have not trained as architects but who have a strong drive to live out something of the fantasy world that they might have had as children. This desire of course often matches that of their clients. One of the better-known American designers is Pete Nelson. As he writes on his web site: "Early on, I had a fascination with and aptitude for working with wood. As a young boy I built a handful of tree houses with my father and my friends and designed my first major tree house while attending high school. It was never built but the tree-house seed was planted." Nelson has not only designed and built numerous tree houses, he also teaches building methods and uses tree houses as a way to get disabled people into nature. Nelson's relative fame is due in good part to the fact that he has published several books. In fact, any cursory search for books about tree houses tends to reveal more and more on the subject, a sure sign that these structures, somehow lodged between reality and fantasy, have struck a chord with popular imagination.

Another interesting figure in tree-house design is Roderick Wolgamott Romero, born in 1965 in Seattle and a presence in the field since the late 1990s. Although Romero has built tree structures for such luminaries as the singer Sting, actors Julianne Moore and Van Kilmer, and fashion designer Donna Karan, he takes a decidedly down-to-earth approach to what he builds, relying almost entirely on salvaged or recuperated materials. He also calls on local craftsmen to participate in his work, which tends to blend into its environment in a seductive way. Perhaps because of his ecological concerns and the way he uses materials, but also because of the very concept of his work, Romero's tree houses seem to sit naturally in the trees where they are built, sometimes recalling a shelter or a nest as much as a real "house." In the work of Roderick Wolgamott Romero it can be seen that there is indeed some distance between the practice of contemporary architecture and that of tree-house design and building, not that the two are mutually exclusive. Romero's tree houses have an element of fantasy in them and a decidedly "green" concept that obviously goes beyond the ecological rhetoric of most architects. Because of the use of recovered materials, mainly wood, and a clearly "low-tech" approach to construction, these structures go back even further in their inspiration than the kind of grand table in the sky imagined by the Medici. This is the lair of the hunter perhaps, but a benign one who only observes nature, a place of refuge in the physical or metaphysical sense, a place to get away from the world.

Because My Companion Is Life Itself

Half a world away from the forests of the West Coast, the Japanese designer Takashi Kobayashi has forged an international reputation for himself, with a joyful, participatory style that has yielded some very spectacular tree houses (for example, Beach Rock Tree House, Okinawa, Japan; page 44). "Sometimes I wonder where I would be now if 16 years ago I had not moved to that small wooden apartment in the back alleys of Harajuku," writes Kobayashi on his web site. "I think about the living Himalaya cedar I found there and the fundamentally different turns my life would surely have taken and can't help but feel the presence of some unseen power. Call it fate, call it what you will. What exactly is it about tree houses that would so captivate a slacker like me, a man who could never devote himself to any one cause or finish anything he started? What is it in tree houses that attracts anyone? I've come to think the answer lies in the vitality of the trees themselves. Everlasting life." Kobayashi's description of his own motivations verges on a nearly spiritual communion with trees and with nature, and, in this, he begins to hint at some of the reasons that tree-house design, construction, and use have become such a widespread phenomena in recent years. "Tree-house building has taken me to forests and woodlands across Japan," he continues, "across the globe, and everywhere I've been, I've seen reflected in these largest and oldest of living beings the same nameless light that I've struggled to maintain within myself for so many years, the one that none could tarnish and that never seemed to disappear. That comfort, that sense of calm, is something I'd like to share with as many people as possible. And it is with that in mind that I will continue with the one-of-a-kind rush that is tree-house creation, all the while carrying out my own personal dialogue with their hosts. Because my companion is life itself. And as long as there are undiscovered trees still waiting…"

A Teahouse Built Too High

In some sense in a very different world than that of the overt communion with nature evoked by Takashi Kobayashi, a number of contemporary architects, much better known for their buildings on the ground than in the trees, have also indulged in tree-house design. The one who might be considered closest to the thoughts of Kobayashi, and not just because he is also Japanese, is Terunobu Fujimori. Born in 1946, Fujimori is a professor at the University of Tokyo's Institute of Industrial Science. He started as a practicing architect quite late by the usual standards, but quickly joined the ranks of the most widely published and influential of Japanese contemporary architects. He plays both on references to Japanese architectural traditions and to the inevitable rapport with nature that such references imply. He has built a number of teahouses, developing on the long and careful thinking that has gone into these structures in Japan, but also venturing, in one instance published here, into Taiwan, where, as he points out, the teahouse is somehow freed of its usual strictures. The Irisentei Tea Nest (Beipu, Taiwan, 2010; page 184) is certainly not a tree house in the usual sense but it is set high off the ground on a giant bamboo trunk. The Takasugi-an or "teahouse (built) too high" (Chino, Nagano, Japan, 2004; page 304) is tiny but makes use of vocabulary that would certainly make observers think of traditional Japanese houses. Framing a view of the town where the architect grew up, this structure has a more defined purpose than many tree houses, and embodies a wry sense of humor that is not always the forte of the designers of "luxury tree houses" seen elsewhere. There are dimensions in the conception and use of Fujimori's tree houses that go beyond what can usually be discovered in the structures designed by people who have a less sophisticated background in architectural history and current events. Clearly stated, Terunobu Fujimori takes the tree house into an entirely different dimension than is normally the case. What he shares with somebody like Kobayashi is an interest in nature, somewhat more sublimated and removed than that of Kobayashi certainly, but the two men share a deep rapport with their country's culture.

Far less well known than Fujimori, Lukasz Kos was born in Starachowice, Poland, in 1978. He studied environmental design at the University of Manitoba (Canada, 2000), obtained a Master of Arts degree in Poland, and then his Master of Architecture degree in Toronto in 2006. His 4Tree House (Walker's Point, Lake Muskoka, Ontario, Canada, 2003; page 34) is a three-story structure that wraps around four trees. This design most certainly leaves the domain of fairy-tale thatched roofs to enter the domain of real, contemporary architecture. And why should tree houses not make that leap?

Aluminum and Mirrored Glass

Perhaps one of the most surprising tree houses published here is the Mirrorcube Tree Hotel, located in Harads (Sweden, 2008; page 238), imagined by the talented architects Bolle Tham (born in 1970) and Martin Videgård (born in 1968). Their firm, Tham & Videgård, created a unique hotel "room" clad in mirrored glass and set up in a tree in the north of Sweden. This four-meter cube is made largely of lightweight aluminum, which is decidedly not the favorite material of most tree-house designers. Plywood is used inside the structure, which has modern comforts like a kitchenette and a double bed. Though the idea of a mirrored aluminum cube has occurred to other architects in the past, a certain leap of the imagination was required to perch such a structure in a tree. The Tree Hotel room gives occupants a 360° view of the forest surroundings and, as such, it immediately breaks from any stereotypical views about Modernist design. Under certain angles this piece of architecture appears to quite simply disappear into its forest surroundings, making an ecological statement, even if modern materials are used as opposed to the hand-hewn wood favored in other tree houses. Placing modern comforts in a tree in such a pure form obviously requires a good deal of architectural design, and immediately places the Tree Hotel in a different category than many other tree houses.

Another very contemporary architectural realization is the Yellow Tree House Restaurant (Warkworth, New Zealand, 2008; page 338) designed by the Auckland architects Pacific Environments. Their 44-square-meter restaurant is located 10 meters above ground level and takes on a seashell-like form. It has a capacity of no less than 18 people including guests and staff. The kitchen and toilet facilities are at ground level for this unique dining place, reached via a 60-meter treetop walkway. "It's the tree house we all dreamed of as children but could only do as an adult fantasy," says designer Peter Eising, echoing a theme that seems very much to be a recurrent one in the world of tree-house design in general. In this instance, the intervention of talented architects clearly gave the Yellow Tree House Restaurant capacities and a level of ambition that could hardly have been reached without real training and modern design and construction methods. Again, though the rather willful lack of sophistication that inhabits many if not most tree houses is clearly absent here, the conjugation of trained architects and the realm of the trees opens new horizons. Users of such a structure are inevitably faced with many of the same sensations as those who climb into a more "traditional" wooden tree house, from the thrill of seeing nature from a new angle to the vertigo related to heights that are conquered using only trees as their main support.

For When the Earth Trembles

Also in New Zealand, the Hapuku Lodge (Kaikoura, South Island; page 160) is run by the Wilson family that counts a number of architects in its number. With their firm Wilson Associates, this family has created tree houses on their property 10 meters off the ground in the midst of Manuka trees. Aside from being visibly architect-designed, these structures are also not tree houses in the usual sense since they are actually propped up on steel girders. The reasoning behind this structure is seismic, but also, of course, allows the designers to create space that affords more of the comforts of modern life than the average wood-and-bolt tree perch. The Wilsons are visibly very much involved in the ecological responsibility of their actions and they are also taking advantage of the strong sensations produced not only by a beautiful natural site, but also by the vertiginous heights usually occupied in such circumstances only by towers or birds' nests. The adaptation of the tree-house form and concept to a more solidly anchored type of architecture is another indication of the hold that the tree house has over the imagination and even the body. Being high in the trees is surely a fantasy of escape and powers over nature that simple humans were not granted. It is a little like flying.

Retro-Future Here We Come

Although tree houses might not seem to be the most obvious form of expression for contemporary artists, there are nonetheless some who are tempted by this genre. One example published in this book is fed by an American counterculture spirit. The Steampunk Tree House (presently located in Milton, Delaware, USA, 2007; page 298) is the work of an artist called Sean Orlando and the Five Ton Crane Arts Group. Its present owner calls it "our off-centered, retro-futuristic sculpture." Created for the 2007 Burning Man festival in Black Rock City, Nevada, this is not really a tree house in the usual sense because it is made of eight tons of recycled and reclaimed materials. Burning

Man is a week-long festival described by its organizers as an "experiment in community, radical self-expression, and radical self-reliance." About 50 000 people attended the event in 2010. Sean Orlando explains that "the Steampunk Tree House was made to explore the relationship between our rapidly changing natural world and the persistent human drive to connect with it and one another. It is our second nature." Although it does assume the form of a tree, the Steampunk Tree House is actually a sculpture. The fact that it uses more metal and other recovered materials than wood is in keeping with Orlando's comment about the "persistent human drive" to connect with nature. Though it does not have real roots, the Steampunk Tree House does in many ways embody the same motivations that have led others, in the United States and elsewhere, to take to the trees.

A second off-beat artist who has built a real tree house is the Swede Mikael Genberg. It was in 1999 that Genberg had the unusual idea to place a little red-and-white house on the moon. In 1999, he heard about the Swedish National Space Board's plans for a new satellite called SMART-1. Imagining that a small house, inspired by traditional Swedish residential architecture, could "symbolize people's faith in the ability to make changes," he created "The House on the Moon Foundation for Mankind" intended to give an annual award "to a person, organization or company that makes earth a better place." Nor did this project exist only in the artist's imagination; he actually designed a structure that could be brought to the moon's surface by an unmanned lunar lander. It is in this context that Genberg also created the Utter Inn, a very small underwater hotel acceded to via a little red house that floats on Lake Mälaren near his hometown of Västerås. In the same vein, the Hackspett Tree House Hotel is also located in Västerås, but 13 meters off the ground. It is again a little red-and-white house, making the link with Mikael Genberg's continuing quest to use this very Swedish symbol as an idea of hope, or perhaps eccentricity, depending on one's point of view. The French artist Jean-Pierre Raynaud long sought to put outsized golden flowerpots in locations from the Forbidden City in Beijing to underwater or outer space locations. His thought process was similar to that of Genberg—an ordinary object as a kind of symbol of hope and regeneration. The Hackspett (Woodpecker) Tree House in itself is an amusing place to spend a night, but in the enlarged context of Mikael Genberg's work and thought process it takes on an added dimension that the average tree-house designer might not have even dreamed of.

Two Nights, Two Dreams

Today, one of the easiest places to discover a tree house is in a "hotel" or resort that features rooms with greater or lesser degrees of comfort, perched high above the ground. These are often not the most sophisticated and architecturally interesting structures, but as they are intended for real, practical use, they certainly have a place in this volume. Given the rising interest in ecologically responsible holidays, and, of course, the demand of vacationers for a real proximity to nature, tree-house hotels are found on every continent, though Europe and Africa seem to have something of a lead over other areas surveyed here.

In France, Natura Cabana offers a number of tree-house rooms in the grounds of the Château Malleret in the Médoc region of France. This is very much a personal project of the person in charge—Prune Gouet, a former sales specialist who created five tree houses without the assistance of an architect, using just a builder and her own sense of forms and ideas about what clients might like. The combination of a fine wine-producing domain close to the tree houses and their own natural setting make Natura Cabana an unusual place to stay. With a plan called "Deux nuits, deux rêves" (two nights, two dreams), Prune Gouet also proposes that clients stay one night in a tree house and one night in the Château Malleret itself. These two very different experiences show that a "tree-house resort" does need to give vacationers a truly unusual and varied stay.

Natura Cabana has had some support from the regional government (Conseil Génerale de la Gironde) and puts a strong emphasis on their own ecological credentials and the responsible nature of tree-house facilities. They also partner with an organization called Bio-organic Holidays.[3]

A similar size venture is Les Nids, located in Le Locle in the Canton of Neuchâtel in Switzerland (page 220). The couple in charge of the facility places an emphasis on the large number of other activities available in the region, ranging from football to cross-country skiing. Though they have a somewhat rustic appearance, Les Nids does offer such "luxuries" as kitchenettes, shower, and toilets, not that common in tree houses elsewhere. As with Natura Cabana, it is the idea of the proximity to nature, or perhaps of cutting off from the more "civilized" world of cities and modern life, that appeals to clients. Tourism, here as in the Médoc region of Natura Cabana, is very much a part of the presentation of the facility made on the web site of Les Nids.

In Sympathy and Connected to Nature

In a rather revealing remark, the American David Greenberg says he studied architecture and urban design before trying "to rebuild Los Angeles after the riots in the early 1990s." He is of a generation that, like some in the 1960s, did their best to start anew and change the world in their own way. He admits to being inspired by the 1970s tree-house experiments in Hawaii and now he has struck out on his own, building tree houses both in Hawaii, and, perhaps even more surprisingly, in China. He has designed the Big Beach in the Sky Tree House (page 64), the Guanyin Tree House, and the Hawaiian Hale Hotel Tree House near the 2000-hectare Sanya Nanshan Buddhist and ecological theme park on the Island of Hainan (China, 2000). With these structures and the ones he has built in Hawaii, Greenberg says he is interested in "creating an architecture that (is) in sympathy and connected to nature particularly in tropical climates." Once again, ecological concerns and an attempt to get closer to nature motivate these efforts. There is a voluntarily picturesque style applied to Greenberg's work, which must surely make reference to realizing childhood dreams as well as adolescent or adult fantasies about escape and the return to a more "authentic" style of life than that afforded by the big cities of the United States or China. The Canopy Tree House (page 90) by Inkaterra, located near Puerto Maldonado in Peru, is a kind of halfway point between a purely ecological project and one that is surely related to tourism. Set in the Inkaterra Reserva Amazonica, a 104-square-kilometer private ecological reserve in the Amazon rain forest, near the Tambopata National Park, a lodge and tree structures arrayed in the Inkaterra Canopy mark this site, weaving between trees that range in height between 30 and 60 meters. A system of bridges, platforms, and towers offers visitors a privileged view into the ecosystems of the rain forest. The ecological diversity of this place is second to none in the world, and visitors are encouraged to come from Miami and elsewhere to stay in the Canopy Tree House. The description of this facility given on the web site of the organization does make it clear that comfort is intended to go here with ecological delights. On its web site, Inkaterra writes: "For the most unique and memorable rainforest experience, Inkaterra's Canopy Tree House offers utter seclusion amidst the splendor of the Peruvian southeastern Amazon. Built on a private platform and adjoining the famous Canopy Walkway at some 90 feet (27 meters) above the lush floor below, the Inkaterra Canopy Tree House provides service that is second to none and a jungle stay like no other. From the remarkable vantage point high in the canopy, guests can observe a range of wild animal species that are not usually visible from the ground, and listen to the amazing jungle sounds whilst unwinding at the relaxing Canopy Bar. Later on guests can soak up the atmosphere over a light dinner watching the stars above before taking a canopy night walk around this remote and fascinating treetop world."[4]

_____ Prowl and Growl

A different approach to being in the wilderness is taken by the private game reserve at Lion Sands (Mpumalanga, South Africa) where guests are given a chance to stay in the nearly legendary Chalkley Tree House (page 96) built on the site where Guy Aubrey Chalkley had set up camp to escape from predators in the 1930s. Chalkley created Lion Sands that year in the Sabi Sand Game Reserve, which is in the Kruger National Park. The designers call it a "bush bedroom," and it is in fact more a platform than a tree house in any traditional sense. It is built around a 500-year-old Leadwood tree. The structure houses a maximum of two people, who are able to view game that is free to wander through the reserve, which has no fences. This proximity to nature again combines the comfort of a soft bed with the bare realities of African wildlife. This is the romantic tree house as refuge from the beasts. In a sense such a structure has less to do with the vertigo of climbing high into a tree and escaping from the bounds of earth than it does with looking down and observing rapidly waning creatures of nature as they prowl and growl.

Lovers of the prowl and growl will also find their happiness at Pezulu Tree House Lodge at Hoedspruit in the province of Limpopo, also in South Africa. There are pilotis-supported structures set between trees, offering such amenities as a bathroom with a Jacuzzi bath. Any of these structures might well have been set on the ground without great surprise, but, perched in the trees, they have the added appeal of being exotic, and also allowing guests to view animals at their leisure. The Honeymoon Tree House at Pezulu Lodge boasts a king-size bed, and a corner sunken bathtub with a view onto a watering hole where giraffes and zebras come to drink.

_____ Do It like the Medici

There is no doubt whatsoever that such structures and facilities are very appealing, but there is a worldwide tendency to "domesticate" the tree house, giving it all the comforts of home, as it were. A sunken bathtub, a plasma-screen television, and designs crafted by top architects are all part of the spectrum of the contemporary tree house. Many of today's structures look curiously like normal houses that may be a bit smaller than usual and are surely less anchored in the earth than they might be. These are signs that the popularity of tree houses in general has led to a bifurcation away from the dreamy refuge from the "real" world that some still endeavor to create. In all fairness, it would appear that centuries ago the Medici did their best to bring all the solidity of

their marble tables and fine food into the trees at Castello and Pratolino. Perhaps the real appeal of tree houses is their very incongruity—the fact that people are not really meant to sit and live in trees. The solidity of the ground is one of the most fundamental sensations, and the tree house often removes that certainty in favor of gentle swaying and doubts about falling. Just as the plays of Shakespeare bring their fated actors into a wood where pretense falls away and reveals another reality, so tree houses are a place to sleep and perhaps to dream. Some tree houses are built in solitary oaks standing near a grand house, but others are deep in the forest, like the aptly named Temple of the Blue Moon published in this book (Issaquah, Washington, USA, 2006; page 316).

The tree house tells a story as old as architecture, or perhaps more clearly, as old as human shelters. To be protected, to escape, and today to find peace and proximity to nature in a world that increasingly denies what used to be part and parcel of existence. The tree house takes on airs of luxury, much like mountain cabins in the Alps and elsewhere have become like five-star hotels rather than the rough places of salvation that they used to be. Hot water flows and Internet is accessible. Even if they are not related to the origins of tree houses, today's structures often appear to ache for simpler times, in some sense for Arcadia. Other structures appear to want the best of both worlds, the innocence of nature before the fall and the comforts of the wide screen.

_____ Cloud-Capp'd Tow'rs and Gorgeous Palaces

In the oeuvre of the French artist Nicolas Poussin, there are two paintings that depict shepherds in Classical dress gathered around a tomb, where the words "Et in Arcadia ego" are inscribed. These words have been translated as "I also was an Arcadian." Related in its origin to the name of a Greek province, the Arcadian myth is one of life in harmony with nature, an idealized life that is quite the contrary of modern "progress." And so, the tree house is about much more than the challenge of climbing and building where there is always the risk of a fall, it is about escape and return. Escape from the pressures of modern life, and return to a simpler life, where the dependency on nature came as a fact of existence. Looking at the tree as the beginning and the end of the story of these castles in the branches is a little like being unable to see the forest for the trees. Though there are all kinds of variants, the story of the tree house is really about the forest, the primeval place of origin. Most often ephemeral and uncertain, tree houses are for some the "cloud-capp'd tow'rs and gorgeous palaces" of which Prospero speaks:

"Our revels now are ended. These our actors, / As I foretold you, were all spirits, and / Are melted into air, into thin air: / And, like the baseless fabric of this vision, / The cloud-capp'd tow'rs, the gorgeous palaces, / The solemn temples, the great globe itself, / Yea, all which it inherit, shall dissolve, / And, like this insubstantial pageant faded, / Leave not a rack behind. We are such stuff / As dreams are made on; and our little life / Is rounded with a sleep." _The Tempest_, Act 4, Scene 1

The tree houses that illustrate this introduction, built by the Korowai people in Irian Jaya (Indonesia), were photographed by the German photographer and explorer Harald Melcher.

1 Anthony Aikman, _Treehouses_, Robert Hale, London, 1988.

2 Anthony Aikman, _Treehouses_, Robert Hale, London, 1988.

3 http://www.bio-organic-holidays.com/ecotourisme/?adherents_id=171 accessed on February 5, 2011.

4 http://www.inkaterra.com/en/reserva-amazonica/canopy-tree-house accessed on February 5, 2011.

auch ich war in arkadien

EINLEITUNG VON PHILIP JODIDIO

Der „Baum des Lebens" oder „Weltenbaum" ist ein Motiv, das sich seit frühester Zeit durch Religion, Philosophie und Mythologie zieht, vom alten Ägypten über China bis hin zum präkolumbischen Mesoamerika. Der in der Erde wurzelnde Baum, dessen Zweige in den Himmel reichen, wurde zum Vorbild für die gotische Architektur. Ohne die Bäume im Wald gäbe es keine Säulen und vielleicht keine Tempel. Der Baum, im Spannungsfeld zwischen Himmel und Erde, ist schon durch seine Größe, Stärke und Langlebigkeit seit jeher ein beeindruckendes Symbol, ein Ort zum Träumen und ein Zufluchtsort. Hoch oben auf einem Baum konnten Menschen aus schwindelerregender Höhe wie ein Vogel im Flug auf das alltägliche Treiben hinabblicken – ein Schritt über die Grenzen des Gewohnten hinaus, eine Ahnung von Unsterblichkeit.

Die Tatsache, dass Baumhäuser in einigen Klimazonen und Kulturen zu den ältesten Formen des Wohnbaus überhaupt zählen, wird durch Völker wie die Kombai und Korowai anschaulich, die in den Ausläufern des Jayawijaya-Gebirges im Südwesten Neuguineas (Indonesien) leben. Ursprünglich wahrscheinlich durch Krankheiten und Stammesrivalitäten bedingt, bauen diese Völker noch heute Baumhäuser in bis zu 40 m Höhe.

Doch Baumhäuser reichen nicht nur in die graue Vorzeit der Geschichte zurück und sind zweifellos eine der frühesten Bauformen schlechthin, sondern finden sich seit der Römerzeit auch in der Geschichte und Kunst Europas. Plinius der Ältere berichtet in seiner *Naturalis historia* (Naturgeschichte) von Caligula, der Kaiser habe auf seinem Anwesen in Velitrae Planken auf die Ästen einer Platane legen und Bänke darauf anbringen lassen, um im Baum rauschende Feste feiern zu können. Auch wissen wir, dass europäische Mönche in der Nähe von Klöstern kleine Einsiedlerklausen in Bäumen bauten; in der Renaissance entstanden in Italien schließlich noch weitaus spektakulärere Baumhausbauten.

Von Caligula bis zum Dominikanermönch

Caligula lebte von 12 v. Chr. bis 41 n. Chr. – doch noch 1500 Jahre später wussten die Mächtigen Italiens Baumhäuser als Zeitvertreib zu nutzen. Cosimo I. de' Medici (1519–1574), erster Herzog der Toskana, ließ für seine toskanische Villa di Castello im Jahr 1538 einen Garten von Niccolò Tribolo gestalten, zu dem auch ein Baumhaus in einer efeubewachsenen Eiche gehörte, in dem er ein quadratisches Speisezimmer einrichten ließ. In seinem Buch *Treehouses* zitiert Anthony Aikman die Beschreibung des Medici-Gartens von Giorgio Vasari:

„Auf einer kleinen Wiese außerhalb des Gartens in östlicher Richtung richtete Tribolo auf höchst kunstvolle Weise einen Eichenbaum her: Dieser ist oben und ringsum zwischen dem Geäst mit Efeuranken bedeckt, was die Wirkung eines sehr dichten Gebüschs erzeugt. Über eine bequeme Holztreppe, die in derselben Weise überwachsen ist, steigt man zu ihm hinauf und gelangt am oberen Ende in einen quadratischen Raum in der Mitte der Eiche, wo sich rundum Bänke und Geländer aus frischen Grünpflanzen befinden. In der Mitte steht auf einem kleinen Marmortisch ein Gefäß aus Buntmarmor. In ihm ist ein Rohr befestigt, aus dem ein kräftiger Wasserstrahl in die Höhe schießt und durch einen weiteren Strahl beim Herabfallen geteilt wird." Die Beschreibung stammt von Vasari, der häufig Besucher in Castello war. Vasari fährt fort: „Diese Röhren [...] sind [...] in einer Weise vom Efeu verdeckt, dass man sie nicht im Geringsten zu erkennen vermag. Der Wasserzufluss wird [...] durch [...] Hebel reguliert. Ich vermag nicht genau zu sagen, über wie viele Wege das Wasser in dieser Eiche zirkuliert und damit diverse Instrumente aus Kupfer in Gang setzt, mit denen man [...] Personen nassspritzen oder auch verschiedene Geräusche und Pfeiftöne erzeugen kann." Höchstwahrscheinlich ließ sich Tribolo von Francesco Colonnas Hypnerotomachia Poliphili [dt. Der Liebestraum des Pholiphilus] inspirieren. In der poetischen Erzählung des Dominikanermönchs Colonna findet sich der Erzähler auf seiner Traumreise durch eine fantastische Landschaft in einer Laube wieder, die aus dem ineinander verschlungenen Geäst eines Obstbaums gebildet wird: „Die Zweige [voll von wundervollem Blattwerk] waren so kunstvoll verwoben und ineinander gewachsen, dass man in ihnen emporsteigen konnte, ohne dass man selbst oder der Weg des Aufstiegs zu sehen war."[1]

Der Eichenbrunnen

Auch Cosimos Sohn Francesco de' Medici (1541–1587) ließ sich ein Baumhaus für seine Villa di Pratolino (Vaglia, Toskana, 1569–1581) entwerfen, das als La Fonte delle Rovere („Der Eichenbrunnen") bekannt wurde: Eine Wendeltreppe führte zu einer 7,5 m hohen Plattform hinauf. Aikman schreibt:

„Um das Baumhaus in Castello zu übertreffen, ließ Francesco nicht nur eine, sondern zwei Treppen um den Stamm der Eiche in Pratolino bauen! Sie wanden sich spiralförmig, auf jeweils gegenüberliegenden Seiten des Baumes parallel zueinander hinauf. Allerdings waren es eher gestufte Rampen als Treppen, die zu einer acht Meter tiefen Plattform führten, die man in die Krone des Baumes hineingebaut hatte. Auf der

Plattform gab es einen Marmortisch, Sitzplätze und Brunnen, die mit Wasser gespeist wurden, das an den Ästen entlang nach oben gepumpt wurde."

Auch Michel de Montaigne (1533–1592) beschrieb Pratolino, das er um 1580 besucht hatte. Der englische Reiseschriftsteller Fynes Moryson (1566–1630) berichtete von einem Baumhaus mit fließendem Wasser, das es in den 1590er-Jahren im schweizerischen Schaffhausen gegeben haben muss, und auch Gemälde von Pieter Bruegel und anderen flämischen Meistern zeugen von Beispielen aus derselben Zeit. Natürlich war auch England ein bedeutender Standort für historische Baumhäuser, darunter so frühe Bauten wie das Baumhaus in Cobham Hall in Kent, das Anfang des 17. Jahrhunderts aus gebogenen Ästen gebaut wurde, oder das bereits 1692 urkundlich erwähnte und noch heute erhaltene Baumhaus in Pitchford Hall bei Shrewsbury in Shropshire. Bereits sehr früh, als der amerikanische Patriot John Ross ein Baumhaus im Garten des Grange Estate in Havertown, Pennsylvania, baute, gelang der sehr europäischen und in gewisser Weise patrizischen Mode für Baumhäuser der Sprung über den Atlantik.[2]

Der schweizerische Robinson und Walt Disney

Auch einige dieser historischen Beispiele haben bereits etwas Mythisch-Fantastisches, doch ab dem 19. Jahrhundert brach eine neue Ära für das Baumhaus an, in der Fakt und Fiktion zusehends verschmolzen. 1845 wurde in der Kleinstadt Le Pessis-Piquet bei Paris das Kabarett *Le grand Robinson* eröffnet, das in drei miteinander verbundenen Baumhäusern untergebracht war. In luftiger Höhe hatten dort bis zu 200 Tische Platz. Seinen Namen verdankte das Kabarett dem 1812 vom schweizerischen Pfarrer Johann David Wyss verfassten Roman *Der Schweizerische Robinson*. Wyss wiederum hatte den höchst unschweizerischen Namen Robinson dem berühmten *Robinson Crusoe* (1712) von Daniel Defoe entlehnt. 1909 wurde das Städtchen Le Plessis-Piquet in Le Plessis-Robinson umbenannt, eine ungewöhnliche Hommage an zwei Romane und ein Kabarett in einem Baumhaus.

Eine unerwartete Wendung sollte dem fiktiven Baumhaus aus *Der Schweizerische Robinson* zu noch größerer Bekanntheit verhelfen. 1960 verfilmte Walt Disney den Roman, und das Baumhaus der Familie Robinson wurde zum festen Bestandteil von Disney-Vergnügungsparks in aller Welt. Die Disney-Version ist dem „echten" Baum zwar nachempfunden, dabei aber ein künstliches Konstrukt aus Stahl, Beton und Putz. Mit 1400 Zweigen, 300 000 Blättern aus Polyethylen und etwas echtem Louisianamoos beweist die Konstruktion, wie populär der Mythos des Baumhauses inzwischen geworden war. Schließlich geht auch der sogenannte „Tree of Life" in Disneys Animal Kingdom [in Florida] auf das Baumhaus des schweizerischen Robinson zurück, greift jedoch auch eines der frühesten Baummotive überhaupt – den Baum des Lebens oder Weltenbaum – auf.

Julia im Küstenmammutbaum

Die Geschichte des Baumhauses wurzelt also im Grunde weit vor Beginn unserer historischen Geschichtsschreibung. So manche Beweggründe für das Errichten frühester Baumhäuser spiegeln sich auch in zeitgenössischen Varianten – etwa das Bedürfnis nach Rückzug, die Nähe zur Natur oder das schwindelerregende Gefühl, hoch über dem Boden zu schweben. Das besonders seit den 1990er-Jahren wachsende Interesse an ökologisch verantwortbaren, nachhaltigen Bauformen

in Europa und den USA hat sicher dazu beigetragen, dass sich mehr und mehr Firmen auf die Gestaltung und den Bau von Baumhäusern spezialisiert haben. Dieser Anstieg reflektiert nicht zuletzt auch ein zunehmendes und anhaltendes öffentliches Interesse an allen nur erdenklichen Arten von Baumhäusern, von schlichten Holzplattformen bis hin zu aufwändigen Wochenenddomizilen mit Plasmafernseher und Alarmanlage. Lebendige, gesunde Bäume sind zweifellos eines der eindrücklichsten Natursymbole, deren Schutz – regelmäßig von radikalen Naturschützern thematisiert – in jüngerer Vergangenheit auch durch eine Art Baumhaus in die Schlagzeilen geriet. Zwischen 1997 und 1999 verbrachte die amerikanische Umweltschützerin Julia „Butterfly" Hill 738 Tage in einem 1500 Jahre alten Küstenmammutbaum auf zwei Plattformen in 60 m Höhe, um die Abholzung des Baums zu verhindern. Ihre Aktion gilt vielen als Höhepunkt des Umweltaktivismus in den USA und wurde in zahlreichen Popsongs aufgegriffen.

Entspannen und Träumen

Ein relativ neues Phänomen der vergangenen zehn bis fünfzehn Jahre ist die wachsende Zahl hoch qualifizierter, kompetenter Gestalter, die sich auf Baumhäuser spezialisiert haben. Einer von ihnen ist der Architekt und gelernte Tischler Andreas Wenning, 1965 in Deutschland geboren. Mit seinem Büro in Bremen realisierte Wenning zahlreiche ausgesprochen zeitgenössische Baumhäuser, von denen einige in diesem Band vorgestellt werden. Der Eingangstext auf Wennings Website vermittelt die besondere Begeisterung und Entdeckerfreude, die Entwürfe seines Büros und anderer zeitgenössischer Baumhausarchitekten auszulösen vermögen: „Ein Baumhaus – ein Erlebnisort für Kinder, Refugium und Rückzug für Erwachsene, ein mit der Natur verbundenes romantisches Kleinod. Diese besonderen, mit Bäumen verbundenen ‚kleinen Häuser' beflügeln die Phantasie und die Neugierde vieler Menschen. Sie wecken in uns Kindheitserinnerungen und den Wunsch, selbst wieder eine Leiter oder Stiege heraufzusteigen und einzutauchen in einen Raum zwischen Ästen und Blattwerk. Sich verzaubern lassen, von den Sinneseindrücken an einem ganz besonderen Ort, im Wandel der Tages- und Jahreszeiten. Ein Ort zum Spielen, zum ungestörten Arbeiten, zum Entspannen und Träumen." Wennings realisierte Projekte sind zweifellos Musterbeispiele der Anwendung gestalterischer und architektonischer Grundprinzipien auf das Baumhaus, doch noch überraschender sind seine unrealisierten Entwürfe mit ihren geradezu avangardistischen Formen. Seine Projekte Winding Snake, Loop oder Cone profitieren zweifellos von seinem Fachwissen über Bäume, sind aber auch erstaunlich aktuell und können durchaus mit dem Standard erdverbundener Bauten mithalten. Obwohl Baumhäuser inzwischen in aller Welt hochmodern und mit technischen Finessen ausgestattet sind, hat sich Wenning gewissermaßen als führender Kopf in der zeitgenössischen Baumhausarchitektur etablieren können.

Eine Brücke, ein Tipi und ein Segelboot

Auch der junge amerikanische Architekt Dustin Feider (O2 Treehouse) beschäftigt sich damit, wie sich modernes Design für Baumhausbauten adaptieren lässt. Er arbeitet mit Materialien wie HDPE (recycelten Plastikflaschen), seine Formen gestaltet er in Anlehnung an Buckminster Fullers geodätische Kuppeln, die bekanntlich mit einem Minimum an Materialaufwand im Verhältnis zum Raumvolumen zu realisieren sind (Seite 148). Sein Entwurf für das Blum Tree House (Hollywood, Kalifornien, USA, 2009) wirkt wie eine Brücke, während das

Tree Pi (Santa Monica, Kalifornien, USA, 2009), ein ebenso schlichtes Design ist, das an ein Tipi erinnert. Feider vertritt mit Anfang Zwanzig fraglos eine neue Generation von Baumhausplanern, die besonderes Verständnis für Formen und ihre Dynamik haben, keine Experimente fürchten und neue Erkenntnisse der zeitgenössischen Architektur auf die Welt der Bäume zu übertragen wissen: Das Prinzip geodätischer Kuppeln etwa lässt sich als Kugelbau aus Dreieckselementen auch als Baumhaus nutzen. Tom Chudleigh hingegen, ein weiterer nordamerikanischer Gestalter, ließ sich vom Bootsbau inspirieren. Seine Free Spirit Spheres (Qualicum Beach, British Columbia, Kanada, Seite 134) schweben an ihrem Standort in British Columbia, Kanada, zwischen Himmel und Erde. Selbst die Aufhängepunkte seiner Baumhaus-Kugeln erinnern an funktionale Details aus dem Segelbootsbau – zweifellos ein gutes Vorbild für ein Objekt, das windbedingten Schwingungen ausgesetzt ist, und dennoch überraschend.

Märchenhafte Luftschlösser

Doch die meisten Baumhausgestalter weltweit distanzieren sich eher vom modernen Stil, für den Andreas Wenning oder Dustin Feider stehen. Sie wollen vielmehr das „Märchenhafte" lebendig halten, das man mit Baumhäusern verbindet. Ein Beispiel sind die oft mit Stroh oder Schindeln gedeckten Baumhäuser des englischen Büros Blue Forest. Für ihr High-Tech Hideaway (Athen, Griechenland, 2004) kombinierten sie ein Reetdach mit Videoüberwachung und Flachbildfernseher. Das innen wie ein Haus mit allem Komfort wirkende Baumdomizil ist offensichtlich ein Kompromiss zwischen moderner Ausstat-

tung und einem Stil, der eher Assoziationen an Sherwood Forest als an Silicon Valley weckt. Der Treetop Dining Room (Leatherhead, Surrey, GB), ebenfalls von Blue Forest, lässt an legendäre historische Baumhäuser Englands oder die Baumhäuser der Medici denken. Es fällt nur allzu leicht, sich hier ein festliches Abendessen in den Bäumen mit berühmten oder weniger berühmten Gästen auszumalen: Hier werden Träume wahr.

Zwei französische Büros verfolgen wiederum andere, höchst ambitionierte Ziele beim Baumhausbau. Das erste Büro, Dans mon Arbre, mit Sitz in Grenoble, gestaltet unter Leitung von Frank Coursier Entwürfe, die in Planung und Realisierung behutsam auf die Bäume abgestimmt sind. Durch die große stilistische Bandbreite des Büros sind die Projekte von Dans mon Arbre nicht immer direkt als solche zu erkennen. Ihr Baumhaus am Château de Langeais (Parc de l'An Mil, Château de Langeais, Frankreich, 2008, Seite 216) ist eine Collage aus verschiedenen Formen und Farben, von der sich viele zeitgenössische Architekten vermutlich distanzieren würden. Gemeinsam mit dem Designer Renaud Morel geht Dans mon Arbre noch etliche Schritte weiter in eine Richtung, die man als grüne Architektur mit hohem Anspruch bezeichnen könnte. Ihr Baumhaus in Kallerput (Eindhoven, Niederlande, 2010, Seite 196) hat stolze 165 m², weit mehr als übliche Baumhäuser. Das sogenannte Village Aérien (dt. Schwebendes Dorf; 2009, Seite 40), ein mit Benoît Fray entwickelter, bisher nicht realisierter Entwurf, besteht aus einer Gruppe freitragender Fachwerkbauten aus Lärchenholz mit einer Wohnfläche von je rund 33 m², die als Hotel geplant sind. Am anderen Ende des Spektrums befinden sich Entwürfe

wie das Boots-Baumhaus (bei Paris, Frankreich, 2009), ein mit einem Budget von 12 000 Euro realisiertes, auf Kinder zugeschnittenes Projekt in einem Ahorn. Bei diesem Baumhaus geht es nicht darum, architektonisch hoch innovativ zu sein, sondern löblicherweise vielmehr darum, Kinder glücklich zu machen – bei vielen hier vorgestellten Baumhäusern die eigentliche Motivation.

Für die Liebe

La Cabane Perchée, ein 2000 von Alain Laurens gegründetes Büro mit Sitz in Südfrankreich, hat sich auf anspruchsvolle, intelligente Entwürfe spezialisiert, die jedoch klar der Formensprache des traditionellen Baumhauses verpflichtet sind. Die im Laub der Bäume verborgenen, oft über steile Wendeltreppen erschlossenen Bauten werden in Zusammenarbeit mit dem Schreinermeister Ghislain André realisiert und sind in erster Linie auf Erwachsene zugeschnitten oder, wie Lau-

rens formuliert „zum Beobachten, Schreiben, Musikhören, Wohlfühlen, zum Träumen, Alleinsein und für die Liebe". Interessanterweise weist Laurens darauf hin, dass Baumhäuser, auch wenn sie für Erwachsene geplant werden, oft ein Kindheitstraum sind – für den Auftraggeber ebenso wie für die Gestalter und Handwerker. Die Entwürfe wurden von den Partnern des Büros in zahlreichen Büchern publiziert, oft begleitet von ansprechenden Aquarellen von Daniel Dufour. La Cabane Perchée hat bisher über 220 Baumhäuser in ganz Europa gebaut, oft für renommierte Auftraggeber, und zählt damit zu den erfahrensten Firmen auf diesem Gebiet.

Trotz des großen Erfolgs bleibt La Cabane Perchée wie die meisten auf Baumhäuser spezialisierten Büros dem Handwerk verpflichtet, im Gegensatz zu einem industrielleren Ansatz, dem Schreinermeister wie Ghislain André eher distanziert gegenüberstehen. Tatsächlich ist fast jedes Baumhaus ein Einzelstück – einer der Gründe, warum sich diese Form von „Architekur" zahlreichen Prämissen widersetzt, die für andere Bauformen gelten. Baumhäuser müssen häufig besonders strengen Auflagen genügen, um eine Baugenehmigung zu erhalten. Dies hängt natürlich davon ab, an welchem Standort sie errichtet werden sollen: Eine simple Tatsache, aufgrund derer sie in die Kategorie „Architektur" fallen, selbst wenn viele der hier vorgestellten Gestalter und Handwerker oft keinen Abschluss als Bauingenieure oder Architekten haben. Schreiner und Baumpfleger sind hier vermutlich stärker vertreten als Architekten im traditionellen Sinne.

Die Baumhaus-Saat ist gesät

Neben Büros unterschiedlicher Größe wie Blue Forest oder La Cabane Perchée sind auch eine Reihe außergewöhnlicher Einzelkünstler auf dem Gebiet der Baumhäuser aktiv. Es sind zumeist Männer, die vielleicht keine Ausbildung als Architekt haben, dafür aber die Vision, Kindheitsträume zu realisieren. Dieser Wunsch deckt sich oft mit dem ihrer Auftraggeber. Einer der bekannteren amerikanischen Baumhaus-Gestalter ist Pete Nelson. Auf seiner Website heißt es: „Ich hatte schon früh ein Faible und Geschick für Holzarbeiten. Als kleiner Junge habe ich mit meinem Vater und meinen Freunden eine Handvoll Baumhäuser gebaut; mein erstes großes Baumhaus entwarf ich, als ich noch auf der Highschool war. Das wurde zwar nie gebaut, doch die Baumhaus-Saat war gesät." Nelson hat nicht nur zahlreiche Baumhäuser entworfen und gebaut, sondern vermittelt auch Baumethoden und bietet Baumhaus-Workshops für Menschen mit Behinderung an, eine Gelegenheit, in die Natur hinauszukommen. Dass Nelson so bekannt ist, verdankt sich auch den zahlreichen Büchern, die er bisher veröffentlicht hat. Tatsächlich macht selbst eine flüchtige Suche nach Büchern über Baumhäuser deutlich, wie viel es zu diesem Thema bereits gibt, ein unverkennbares Zeichen, dass sich diese zwischen Fantasie und Wirklichkeit angesiedelten Bauten offensichtlich einen Platz in unseren Köpfen erobert haben. Ein weiterer faszinierender Baumhausgestalter ist Roderick Romero, 1965 in Seattle geboren, und seit Ende der 1990er-Jahre auf diesem Gebiet sehr aktiv. Obwohl Romero Baumhäuser für so bekannte Persönlichkeiten wie Sting, Julianne Moore, Val Kilmer oder Donna Karan gebaut hat, sind seine Entwürfe doch erstaunlich bodenständig – er baut fast nur mit recycelten oder Altmaterialien. Außerdem arbeitet er mit ortsansässigen Handwerkern. Seine Entwürfe integrieren sich oft gelungen in ihr Umfeld. Es mag an seinem Verständnis für ökologische Belange und seinem Einsatz von Altmaterialien liegen, dass sich seine Häuser wie selbstverständlich in die Bäume fügen, in die sie hineingebaut wurden. Mitunter erinnern sie eher an einen Unterstand oder ein Nest als an richtige „Häuser". An den Entwürfen von Roderick Romero wird deutlich, dass es tatsächlich große Unterschiede zwischen zeitgenössischer Architekturpraxis und dem Entwurf und Bau von Baumhäusern gibt, auch wenn sich beide durchaus nicht ausschließen müssen. Romeros Baumhäuser haben etwas Fantastisches und zeugen von einer „grünen" Philosophie, die weit über die ökologischen Gesten der meisten Architekten hinausgeht. Mit ihren recycelten Materialien, zumeist aus Holz, und dem offensichtlichen „Low-Tech"-Ansatz verweisen diese Baumhäuser historisch wesentlich weiter zurück als auf die schwebenden, hochherrschaftlichen Banketttafeln der Medici. Referenzen sind hier eher die Höhlen von Jägern, freundlichen Jägern, die die Natur beobachten; ein Zufluchtsort im realen wie im metaphysischen Sinne, ein Ort um der Welt zu entfliehen.

Mein Gefährte ist das Leben selbst

Ein halbe Weltreise von den Wäldern der amerikanischen Westküste entfernt hat sich der Japaner Takashi Kobayashi mit seinem heiteren, partizipatorischen Stil einen internationalen Ruf als Baumhausgestalter erworben: Entstanden sind auf diese Weise einige spektakuläre Bauten. „Manchmal frage ich mich, wo ich heute wäre, wenn ich nicht vor 16 Jahren in die kleine Holzwohnung in den versteckten Gassen von Harajuku gezogen wäre", schreibt Kobayashi auf seiner Website. „Ich muss an die Himalaya-Zeder denken, die ich dort entdeckt habe und an die fundamental andere Richtung, in die sich mein Leben sonst zweifellos entwickelt hätte, und ich kann nicht anders, als hinter all dem eine unsichtbare Kraft zu vermuten. Nennen wir sie Schicksal oder wie immer wir wollen. Was haben Baumhäuser nur, dass sie einen Herumtreiber wie mich so faszinieren, jemanden, der nie bei etwas bleiben konnte, der nie etwas fertig gebracht hat, was er angefangen hatte. Wieso faszinieren Baumhäuser überhaupt irgend jemanden? Ich bin für mich zu dem Schluss gekommen, dass die Antwort in der Lebenskraft der Bäume liegt. Ewiges Leben." Die Art, wie Kobayashi über seine Beweggründe spricht, hat geradezu etwas Spirituelles, etwas von einer Vereinigung mit den Bäumen, der Natur. Damit rührt er an einen der Gründe, warum sich das Gestalten und Bauen von Baumhäusern in den vergangenen Jahren zu einem so verbreiteten Phänomen entwickelt hat. „Das Bauen von Baumhäusern hat mich in Wälder und Waldgebiete in ganz Japan geführt", erzählt er weiter, „und um die ganze Welt. Und wohin auch immer es mich verschlug, sah ich in diesen größten und ältesten Lebewesen dasselbe namenlose Licht, das ich über die Jahre in mir selbst wachzuhalten versucht habe, jenes Licht, das niemand trüben kann und das nie zu schwinden scheint. Dieser Trost, dieses Gefühl der Ruhe ist etwas, das ich mit so vielen Menschen wie möglich teilen möchte. Mit diesen Gedanken im Kopf werde ich weiter diesem einzigartigen Rausch nachjagen, Baumhäuser zu bauen und dabei mein privates Zwiegespräch mit ihren ‚Wirten' weiterspinnen. Denn mein Gefährte ist das Leben selbst. Und solange es noch unentdeckte Bäume gibt..."

Ein Teehaus, zu hoch gebaut

Eine ganz andere Welt als das demonstrative Verschmelzen mit der Natur, das Takashi Kobayashi vertritt, sind die Baumhausentwürfe verschiedener zeitgenössischer Architekten, die für ihre erdverbundenen Bauten ungleich bekannter sind als für ihre Baumhäuser. Einer von ihnen, der Kobayashis Philosophie vielleicht am nächsten steht, und das nicht nur, weil auch er Japaner ist, ist Terunobu Fujimori. Fujimori, Jahrgang 1946, ist Professor am Institut für Ingenieurwissenschaften der Universität Tokio. Er begann ungewöhnlich spät, als Architekt zu arbeiten, doch etablierte er sich rasch als einer der meistpublizierten und einflussreichsten zeitgenössischen Architekten Japans. Fujimori spielt sowohl mit Referenzen zu traditionellen japanischen Baustilen als auch mit Bezügen zur Natur, die solche Referenzen zwangsläufig mit sich bringen. Er hat eine Reihe von Teehäusern realisiert und knüpft dabei an die vielschichtige Tradition dieser Bauten in Japan an. Bei dem hier vorgestellten Projekt in Taiwan jedoch befreite er das Teehaus, wie er selbst sagt, von landläufigen Vorstellungen. Das Irisentei Tea Nest, (Beipu, Taiwan, 2010, Seite 184) ist ohne Frage kein Baumhaus im üblichen Sinne, schwebt jedoch hoch auf einem mächtigen Bambusstamm. Das Takasugi-an, was so viel heißt wie ein „Teehaus, zu hoch (gebaut)" (Chino, Nagano, Japan, 2004, Seite 304) ist winzig, dabei aber einer Formensprache verpflichtet, die unmittelbar Assoziationen an japanische Architektur weckt. Das Teehaus mit Blick auf das Städtchen, in dem der Architekt aufgewachsen ist, hat eine weitaus spezifischere Funktion als die meisten Baumhäuser und zeugt zugleich von einem trockenen Humor, der nicht unbedingt die Stärke vieler Planer „luxuriöser Baumhäuser" ist, wie sich andernorts zeigt. Konzeption und Zweck der Baumhäuser Fujimoris sind ungleich überzeugender und facettenreicher als vergleichbare Bauten anderer Gestalter, die weniger Hintergrund in Architekturgeschichte haben und weniger vertraut mit zeitgenössischen Entwicklungen sind. Anders gesagt, öffnen Terunobu Fujimoros Baumhäuser vollkommen andere Dimensionen, als Baumhäuser dies landläufig tun. Was ihn mit Kobayashi verbindet, ist das Interesse an der Natur, zweifellos indirekter und distanzierter als bei Kobayashi – dennoch teilen die beiden Männer eine große Verbundenheit zur Kultur ihres Heimatlandes.

Wesentlich weniger bekannt als Fujimori ist Lukasz Kos, 1978 in Starachowice, Polen, geboren. Er studierte Umweltgestaltung an der Universität von Manitoba (Kanada, 2000), schloss zunächst ein Kunststudium in Polen und schließlich 2006 ein Architekturstudium in Toronto (M.Arch.) ab. Sein 4Tree House (Walker's Point, Lake Muskoka Ontario, Kanada, 2003, Seite 34) ist eine dreistöckige Konstruktion, die auf vier Bäumen ruht. Dieser Entwurf ist zweifellos alles andere als ein märchenhafter Reetdachbau, vielmehr fest verankert in der Welt der zeitgenössischen Architektur. Doch warum sollten Baumhäuser diesen Sprung auch nicht wagen?

Aluminium und Spiegelglas

Eines der erstaunlichsten Baumhäuser in diesem Band ist sicherlich das Mirrorcube Tree Hotel in Harads (Schweden, 2008, Seite 238), ein Entwurf der bemerkenswerten Architekten Bolle Tham (geb. 1970) und Martin Videgård (geb. 1968). Mit ihrem Büro Tham & Videgård realisierten die beiden ein einzigartiges „Einzimmer-Hotel" in einem Baum. Die mit Spiegelglas verkleidete Konstruktion liegt in Nordschweden. Der 4 x 4 m große Kubus besteht vorwiegend aus besonders leichtem Aluminium, was definitiv nicht zu den favorisierten Materialien der meisten Baumhausgestalter zählt. Im Innern des mit modernem Komfort wie einer Kleinküche und einem Doppelbett ausgestatteten Würfels wurde Schichtholz verbaut. Zwar ist das Motiv des verspiegelten Aluminiumkubus in der Vergangenheit bereits bei anderen Architekten zu sehen gewesen, doch war es ein kreativer Sprung, die Konstruktion in einen Baum zu versetzen. Vom Tree Hotel haben die Besucher Rundumblick in die waldige Umgebung – sicher ein Kontrast zu gängigen Klischeevorstellungen von modernem Design. Aus bestimmten Blickwinkeln ist das Bauwerk so gut wie unsichtbar inmitten der Bäume: Ein ökologisches Statement, auch wenn hier keineswegs mit rustikalem Holz gebaut wurde, Material der Wahl bei vielen anderen Baumhäusern. Modernem Wohnkomfort eine so schlichte Form zu geben und in einen Baum zu versetzen erfordert ein erhebliches Maß an architektonischer Planung und Gestaltung. Entsprechend spielt das Tree Hotel ohne Frage in einer anderen Liga als viele andere Baumdomizile.

Eine ebenfalls ausgesprochen zeitgenössische Architektur ist das Yellow Tree House Restaurant (Warkworth, Neuseeland, 2008, Seite 338) von Pacific Environments in Auckland. Ihr 44 m² großes, an eine Muschel erinnerndes Restaurant schwebt 10 m über dem Boden. Es bietet Platz für nicht weniger als 18 Personen (Gäste und Service-

personal). Küche und Toiletten dieses ungewöhnlichen Restaurants liegen ebenerdig. Erschlossen wird das Restaurant über eine 60 m lange Rampe zwischen den Bäumen. „Es ist genau das Baumhaus, von dem wir als Kinder geträumt haben, eine Fantasie, die wir erst als Erwachsene realisieren konnten", sagt Architekt Peter Eising und greift damit ein Thema auf, das sich wie ein Leitmotiv durch die Welt der Baumhäuser zu ziehen scheint. Wie dieses Bespiel zeigt, verdankt das Yellow Tree House Restaurant der Planung fähiger Architekten eine räumliche Großzügigkeit und einen Anspruch, die ohne entsprechende Ausbildung und Kenntnisse moderner Gestaltungs- und Konstruktionsmethoden definitiv nicht realisierbar gewesen wären. Hier ist von jenem bewussten Verzicht auf Perfektion, der viele, wenn nicht gar die meisten Baumhäuser auszeichnet, nichts zu spüren, stattdessen öffnet das vielseitige Können qualifizierter Architekten im Kontext der Bäume neue Horizonte.. Trotzdem löst ein solcher Bau bei Besuchern in vielerlei Hinsicht dieselben Empfindungen aus wie der Aufstieg in ein „traditionelleres" Baumhaus: vom Reiz, die Natur aus einem neuen Blickwinkel zu sehen, bis hin zum Schwindelgefühl, das einen beim Erklimmen hoher Bäumen beschleicht.

Wenn die Erde bebt

Die Hapuku Lodge (Kaikoura, Südinsel, Neuseeland, Seite 160) der Familie Wilson, zu der auch einige Architekten gehören, liegt ebenfalls in Neuseeland. Mit ihrem Büro Wilson Associates realisierte die Familie auf ihrem Grundstück zwischen Manuka-Bäumen Baumhäuser in 10 m Höhe. Diese Bauten sind keine Baumhäuser im strengen Wortsinn, sondern ruhen vielmehr auf Stahlträgern. Die Gründe für diese Entscheidung liegen in der Erdbebengefahr in der Region, zugleich erlaubten sie den Architekten, Räume zu planen, die wesentlich mehr Komfort bieten als sonst an Bäumen fixierte „Hochsitze". Ganz offensichtlich ist ökologische Verantwortung den Wilsons ein großes Anliegen. Dabei wissen sie nicht nur die emotionale Wirkung der außergewöhnlich schönen landschaftlichen Umgebung zu nutzen, sondern auch die schwindelerregende Höhe der Bauten, eine Höhe, die man sonst nur von Türmen oder Vogelnestern kennt. Die Tendenz, den Baumhaustypus in formaler wie konzeptueller Hinsicht auf beständigere Bauformen zu übertragen, ist ein weiteres Indiz dafür, welche Faszination das Baumhaus auf unsere Vorstellungskraft, wenn nicht gar rein physisch auf uns ausübt. Hoch in den Baumwipfeln zu schweben ist ohne Frage eine Flucht- und Machtfantasie, die dem Menschen sonst nicht erfüllt wird – eine Ahnung vom Fliegen.

Retro-Futurismus

Für zeitgenössische Künstler sind Baumhäuser sicher nicht das naheliegendste Medium, und doch gibt es einige, die dieses Genre reizt. Zwei Beispiele finden sich in diesem Band – eines ist inspiriert von der amerikanischen Gegenkultur, ein anderes von einem schwedischen Baum. Das Steampunk Tree House (zurzeit in Milton, Delaware, USA, 2007, Seite 298) ist eine Kollaboration des Künstlers Sean Orlando mit der Five Ton Crane Arts Group. Der aktuelle Besitzer nennt das Baumhaus eine „exzentrische, retro-futuristische Skulptur". Die Skulptur, 2007 für das Burning Man Festival in Black Rock City, Nevada, entworfen, ist kein Baumhaus im üblichen Sinne und besteht aus acht Tonnen Recycling- und Altmaterialien. Das Burning Man Festival, ein „Experiment in Sachen Gemeinschaft, radikalem Selbstausdruck und radikaler Eigenverantwortlichkeit" hatte 2010 rund 50 000 Besucher.

Sean Orlando versteht das „Steampunk Tree House als Auseinandersetzung mit unserer sich rasend verändernden Umwelt und dem unverbrüchlichen menschlichen Bedürfnis, den Kontakt zur Natur und zueinander zu suchen. Das ist unser natürlicher Instinkt." Obwohl einem Baum nachempfunden, ist das Steampunk Tree House eher eine Skulptur. Die Tatsache, dass mehr Metall und andere Altmaterialien verbaut wurden als Holz, ist ein geradezu ironischer Kommentar zu Orlandos These vom „unverbrüchlichen menschlichen Bedürfnis", den Kontakt zur Natur zu suchen. Obwohl das Steampunk Tree House keine echten Wurzeln hat, verkörpert es dennoch in vielerlei Hinsicht dieselben Bedürfnisse und Motivationen, die Menschen in den USA und an anderen Orten dazu bringt, sich Bäumen zuzuwenden.

Ein anderer Künstler jenseits des Mainstreams, der das Baumhaus-Motiv aufgreift, ist der Schwede Mikael Genberg. 1999 kam Genberg der ungewöhnliche Gedanke, ein kleines rot-weißes Haus auf den Mond zu schicken, als er von den Plänen der schwedischen Weltraumbehörde für einen neuen Satelliten, den SMART-1, hörte. Genberg war der Ansicht, ein kleines Haus, inspiriert von der traditionellen schwedischen Architektur, könne ein „Symbol für den Glauben des Menschen an Veränderung" sein. Er gründete die „Haus-auf-dem-Mond-Stiftung

für die Menschheit", die jedes Jahr einen Preis an „eine Persönlichkeit, Organisation oder ein Unternehmen" verleihen soll, „die die Welt zu einem besseren Ort machen". Doch sein Projekt ist nicht etwa rein fiktiv, er plante tatsächlich ein Haus, das mit einer unbemannten Mondfähre auf den Mond gebracht werden könnte. In diesem Zusammenhang entwarf Genberg auch ein winziges Unterwasserhotel, das Utter Inn. Zugang erhält man über ein kleines rotes Schwedenhaus, das auf dem Mälarsee, unweit seiner Heimatstadt Västerås schwimmt. Nach demselben Prinzip konzipierte er auch das Kleinst-Baumhaushotel Hackspett in Västerås, das 13 m über dem Boden schwebt. Auch dieses Haus ist ein kleines rot-weißes Schwedenhaus, und damit ein weiterer Bogenschlag zu Mikael Genbergs unermüdlichem Bemühen, dieses so typisch schwedische Symbol als Hoffnungsträger (oder, je nach Standpunkt, als Zeichen für eine gewisse Exzentrik) zu nutzen. Ein anderes Beispiel ist der französische Künstler Jean-Pierre Raynaud, der im Rahmen eines Langzeitprojekts immer wieder übergroße goldene Blumentöpfe an den unterschiedlichsten Orten platzierte, von der Verbotenen Stadt über Orte unter Wasser bis hin zum Weltraum. Sein Ansatz war ähnlich wie der von Genberg – ein gewöhnliches Objekt wird zum Symbol der Hoffnung und Erneuerung erhoben. Das Hackspett (Specht) Baumhaus ist sicherlich ein charmanter Ort für eine Nacht, doch im Kontext von Mikael Genbergs Werk und konzeptuellem Ansatz gewinnt es eine zusätzliche Dimension, von der die meisten Baumhausgestalter nicht zu träumen wagen.

Zwei Nächte, zwei Träume

Die einfachste Möglichkeit, heutzutage ein Baumhaus zu entdecken, ist der Aufenthalt in einem Hotel oder einer Ferienanlage, die Zimmer mit mehr oder weniger Komfort hoch über dem Boden anbieten. Oft sind dies nicht die anspruchsvollsten oder architektonisch interessantesten Bauten, doch dafür sind sie ganz auf die reale, praktische Nutzung zugeschnitten und haben zweifellos ihren Platz in diesem Band verdient. Angesichts des wachsenden Interesses an ökologisch nachhaltigen Urlaubsangeboten und dem Wunsch von Urlaubern nach echter Nähe zur Natur finden sich solche Baumhaushotels inzwischen auf allen Kontinenten. Europa und Afrika jedoch scheinen hier eine Vorreiterrolle einzunehmen.

Die Anlage Natura Cabana in Frankreich bietet gleich eine ganze Reihe von Baumhäusern mit Hotelzimmern und liegt auf dem Grundstück des Château Malleret in der Region Médoc. Das Projekt ist in erster Linie die Initiative einer Einzelperson – Prune Gouet, einer ehemaligen Vertriebsspezialistin, die ihre fünf Baumhäuser ohne Unterstützung eines Architekten realisierte, ausschließlich mit Hilfe eines Bauunternehmers und mit ihrem eigenen Gefühl für Formen und ihrer Vorstellung davon, was ihren Gästen gefallen könnte. Ein besonders ungewöhnlicher Ort sind die Baumhäuser Natura Cabana auch durch ihre Nähe zu einem gehobenen Weingut und durch die landschaftliche Umgebung. Mit ihrem Urlaubspaket „Deux nuits, deux rêves" (zwei Nächte, zwei Träume) bietet Prune Gouet ihren Gästen einen zweitägigen Aufenthalt an: eine Nacht im Baumhaus, eine zweite Nacht im Hauptgebäude des Château Malleret. Diese beiden so unterschiedlichen Erlebnisse machen deutlich, dass eine „Baumhaus-Ferienanlage" durchaus gut daran tut, ihren Gästen einen wirklich ungewöhnlichen und abwechslungsreichen Aufenthalt zu bieten. Das Natura Cabana wird von der Region gefördert (dem Conseil Génerale de la Gironde) und legt besonderen Wert auf seine ökologischen Referenzen sowie eine nachhaltige Bauweise. Die Anlage kooperiert mit der Organisation „Bio-organic Holidays".[3]

Eine ähnliche Anlage ist Les Nids in Le Locle im schweizerischen Kanton Neuchâtel. Das Inhaberpaar legt besonderen Wert auf die vielfältigen Freizeitaktivitäten der Region, von Fußball bis hin zum Skilanglauf. Trotz ihres eher rustikalen Flairs verfügt Les Nids über Komfort wie Küchenzeilen, Duschen und Toiletten, eher ungewöhnlich für Baumhäuser anderer Anbieter. Wie bei Natura Cabana ist es auch hier die Nähe zur Natur, wenn nicht gar die Distanz zur „Zivilisation" der Städte und des modernen Lebens, die die Gäste besonders reizt. Bei der Werbung für Les Nids steht der Tourismus ebenso im Vordergrund wie bei der Natura Cabana oder der Region Médoc.

Rücksicht und Gespür für die Natur

Die Aussage des Amerikaners David Greenberg, er habe Architektur und Stadtplanung studiert, um schließlich „in den frühen 1990er-Jahren nach den Aufständen für den Wiederaufbau von Los Angeles" zu arbeiten, ist recht aufschlussreich. Greenberg gehört zu jener Generation, die sich wie manche andere in den 1960er-Jahren für einen Neuanfang engagierten und dafür, die Welt in ihrem Sinne zu verän-

dern. Inspiration waren für ihn unter anderem die Baumhaus-Aktionen der 1970er-Jahre auf Hawaii. Inzwischen hat Greenberg seine eigene Firma, mit der er Baumhäuser auf Hawaii und überraschenderweise auch in China baut. Zu seinen Projekten zählen das Baumhaus Big Beach in the Sky (Seite 64), das Guanyin-Baumhaus und das Baumhaushotel Hawaiian Hale in der Nähe des 2000 ha großen buddhistischen ökologischen Sanya-Nanshan-Freizeitparks auf der Insel Hainan (China, 2000). Mit diesen Bauten und weiteren Projekten auf Hawaii geht es Greenberg nach eigener Aussage darum, „eine Architektur zu schaffen, die von Rücksicht und Gespür für die Natur geprägt ist, insbesondere in tropischen Klimaregionen". Auch hier ist die Triebfeder wiederum ein ökologisches Bewusstsein und der Wunsch nach größerer Nähe zur Natur. Greenbergs Entwürfe haben etwas bewusst Malerisches, wirken zweifellos wie die Erfüllung von Kindheits-, Jugend- oder gar Erwachsenenträumen, wie eine Flucht aus dem Alltag und die Rückkehr zu einem Lebensstil, der „authentischer" ist, als dies in den großen Städten Amerikas oder Chinas realisierbar ist.

Das Canopy Tree House (Seite 92) in der Ferienanlage Inkaterra bei Puerto Maldonado in Peru ist einerseits ein ökologisches Projekt, andererseits eindeutig touristisch orientiert. Die inmitten der Reserva Amazonica, einem 104 km^2 großen privaten Naturschutzgebiet gelegene Inkaterra-Ferienanlage unweit des Tambopata Nationalparks besteht aus einem Haupthaus und verschiedenen Baumhausbauten, die in den 30 bis 60 m hohen Bäumen verteilt sind. Brücken, Terrassen und Türme verbinden die Bauten und bieten den Besuchern außergewöhnliche Einblicke in das Ökosystem des Regenwalds. Die ökologische Vielfalt des Orts ist unvergleichlich, Besucher reisen für ihren Aufenthalt im Canopy Tree House aus Miami und anderen Städten an. Die Darstellung der Anlage im Internet lässt keinen Zweifel daran, dass man hier Komfort mit einem besonderen Naturerlebnis zu verbinden weiß. Auf der Website von Inkaterra heißt es: „Das Canopy Tree House von Inkaterra bietet ein außergewöhnliches und unvergessliches Regenwald-Erlebnis in absoluter Abgeschiedenheit inmitten des großartigen Amazonas-Gebiets im Südosten Perus. Gelegen auf einer privaten Plattform und in unmittelbarer Nachbarschaft zum berühmten Canopy Walkway in rund 27 m Höhe über dem üppigen Dschungelboden, bietet das Inkaterra Canopy Tree House unvergleichlichen Service und ein Dschungelerlebnis, das seinesgleichen sucht. Aus dem ungewöhnlichen Blickwinkel in Höhe des Blätterdachs können die Gäste zahlreiche wilde Tierarten beobachten, die vom Boden aus sonst nicht zu sehen sind, den faszinierenden Klangwelten des Dschungels lauschen und dabei an der Canopy Bar entspannen. Später können sie die Atmosphäre bei einem leichten Dinner auf sich wirken lassen, die Sterne über sich betrachten und schließlich einen nächtlichen Spaziergang auf dem Canopy Walk inmitten der entlegenen und faszinierenden Welt zwischen den Baumwipfeln unternehmen."[4]

Auf der Wildpirsch

Eine andere Philosophie vom Leben in der Wildnis verfolgt der private Wildpark Lion Sands (Mpumalanga, Südafrika), wo Gäste im legendären Chalkley Tree House (Seite 96) wohnen können, das genau dort errichtet wurde, wo Guy Aubrey Chalkley in den 1930er-Jahren in seinem Lager Zuflucht vor den Raubtieren suchte. Damals gründete Chalkley den Park Lion Sands im Wildschutzgebiet Sabi Sand, dem heutigen Kruger Nationalpark. Die Planer nennen das Chalkley Tree House ein „Schlafzimmer im Busch" und tatsächlich ist es eher eine erhöhte Terrasse als ein Baumhaus im üblichen Sinne. Erbaut um einen fünfhundertjährigen Leadwood-Baum, bietet die Plattform Platz für zwei Gäste, die von hier aus das frei lebende Wild im Park beobachten können. Hier verbindet sich die Nähe zur Natur mit dem Komfort eines weichen Betts und der realen Lebenswelt der afrikanischen Tierwelt: Das Baumhaus als romantischer Zufluchtsort vor wilden Tieren. Hier geht es weniger um den schwindelerregenden Aufstieg in einen hohen Baum oder die Überwindung der Erdanziehungskraft als um den Blick nach unten, das Beobachten allzu rasch aussterbender Wildtiere auf der Pirsch.

Liebhaber der Wildpirsch dürften auch in der Pezulu Tree House Lodge in Hoedspruit in der Provinz Limpopo, ebenfalls in Südafrika, glücklich werden. Die auf Pilotis schwebenden Bauten liegen zwischen Bäumen und sind mit höchstem Komfort wie Badezimmern mit Jacuzzi ausgestattet. Zweifellos hätten diese Pavillons ebenso gut auf dem Boden errichtet werden können, doch in den Bäumen gewinnen sie an exotischem Reiz und erlauben den Gästen darüber hinaus das entspannte Beobachten der Tiere. Das Honeymoon Tree House der Pezulu Lodge verfügt über ein großes Doppelbett und eine in den Boden eingelassene Badewanne mit Blick auf ein Wasserloch, an dem Giraffen und Zebras zur Tränke kommen.

Wie die Medici

Ohne Frage haben solche Bauten ihren Reiz, doch scheint sich weltweit der Trend durchzusetzen, das Baumhaus zu „domestizieren", es mit dem Komfort eines echten Wohnhauses auszustatten. Zur Bandbreite zeitgenössischer Baumhäuser gehören heute eben auch in den Boden eingelassene Badewannen, Plasmafernseher und von Stararchitekten entworfene Designs. Heute ähneln viele Baumhäuser auffällig regulären Wohnbauten – sind vielleicht etwas kleiner und sicherlich weniger erdverbunden als gewohnt. Dies alles sind Zeichen, dass die Popularität von Baumhäusern auch dazu geführt hat, dass sich dieser Typus immer stärker von jenem träumerischen Zufluchtsort vom Alltag entfernt, den manche nach wie vor schaffen wollen. Doch auch die Medici taten schon vor Jahrhunderten alles, was in ihrer Macht stand, um ihre massiven Marmortische und feinen Speisen in die Bäume von Castello und Pratolino zu verlegen. Vielleicht liegt der wahre Reiz des Baumhauses in eben dieser Diskrepanz – dass Menschen eigentlich nicht dafür gemacht sind, auf Bäumen zu sitzen oder zu wohnen. Der feste Boden unter uns ist eine unserer fundamentalsten Erfahrungen, die uns das Baumhaus entzieht, um uns stattdessen sanftes Wiegen und die Angst vor dem Fallen zu bescheren. So wie Shakespeare seine schicksalhaften Figuren in den Wald führt, der jeden Schein entlarvt und eine tiefere Wahrheit zum Vorschein bringt, so sind auch Baumhäuser Orte, um zu schlafen, vielleicht zu träumen. Manche Baumhäuser liegen in einsamen Eichen bei herrschaftlichen Villen, andere tief im Wald, wie der ebenfalls in diesem Band vorgestellte, poetisch betitelte Temple of the Blue Moon (Issaquah, Washington, USA, 2006, Seite 316).

Das Baumhaus erzählt eine Geschichte, die so alt ist wie die Architektur selbst, oder vielleicht so alt wie die menschliche Behausung schlechthin. Es geht um Schutz, um Flucht, darum, heute – in einer Welt, die uns zunehmend vorenthält, was früher selbstverständlicher Bestandteil der menschlichen Existenz war – einen friedlichen Ort zu finden, in Nähe zur Natur. Inzwischen gibt sich das Baumhaus luxuriös, genau wie die Berghütte in den Alpen, die heute eher Fünf-Sterne-Hotels ähnelt als jenen einfachen Schutzhütten, auf die sie zurückgeht.

Hier gibt es fließendes Wasser und Internetzugang. Auch wenn manche Baumhäuser heute nicht mehr viel mit ihren Urformen verbindet, zeugen sie dennoch von der Sehnsucht nach dem Einfachen, nach unkomplizierteren Zeiten, nach Arkadien. Wieder andere Baumhäuser scheinen beide Welten verbinden zu wollen: Die Unschuld der unberührten Natur mit den Annehmlichkeiten des Breitbildfernsehers.

Die wolkenhohen Türme, die Paläste

Im Werk des französischen Malers Nicolas Poussin finden sich zwei Gemälde mit dem Titel *Die Hirten von Arkadien*: Hirten in klassischen Gewändern vor einem Grabmal, auf das die Worte „Et in Arcadia ego" eingeschrieben sind – „Auch ich war in Arkadien". In Anlehnung an die griechische Landschaft, der sie ihren Namen verdankt, gilt Arkadien in der Mythologie als Ort der Harmonie mit der Natur, als Ort eines idealen Lebens, das sich nicht stärker vom modernen „Fortschritt" unterscheiden könnte. In diesem Sinne ist das Baumhaus weit mehr als die Herausforderung, hinaufzusteigen und zu bauen, wo man auch fallen kann: Es geht um Flucht und Rückkehr. Flucht vor den Zwängen des modernen Lebens und Rückkehr zu jenem einfacheren Leben, in dem das Angewiesensein auf die Natur einst existentielles Erfordernis war. Doch den Baum als Ursprung und Ziel dieser in die Wipfel gebauten Schlösser zu begreifen, würde bedeuten, den Wald vor lauter Bäumen nicht zu sehen. Trotz seiner zahlreicher Spielarten geht es bei der Geschichte des Baumhauses im Grunde um den Wald, den urzeitlichen Ursprungsort. Und schließlich sind die oft flüchtigen, unsicheren Baumhäuser für manche eben jene „wolkenhohen Türme, die Paläste", von denen Prospero spricht:

„Das Fest ist jetzt zu Ende; unsre Spieler,
Wie ich Euch sagte, waren Geister, und
Sind aufgelöst in Luft, in dünne Luft.
Wie dieses Scheines lockrer Bau, so werden
Die wolkenhohen Türme, die Paläste,
Die hehren Tempel, selbst der große Ball,
Ja, was daran nur Teil hat, untergehn
Und, wie dies leere Schaugepräng' erblasst,
Spurlos verschwinden. Wir sind solcher Zeug
Wie der zu Träumen und dies kleine Leben
Umfasst ein Schlaf."

Der Sturm, Vierter Aufzug, Erste Szene

Die Baumhäuser, gebaut von den Korowai in Irian Jaya (Indonesien), die diese Einleitung illustrieren, wurden von dem deutschen Fotografen und Entdecker Harald Melcher aufgenommen.

1 Anthony Aikman, *Treehouses*, London 1988.
2 Anthony Aikman, *Treehouses*, London 1988.
3 http://www.bio-organic-holidays.com/ecotourisme/?adherents_id=171, Zugriff am 5. Februar 2011.
4 http://www.inkaterra.com/en/reserva-amazonica/canopy-tree-house, Zugriff am 5. Februar 2011.

et in arcadia ego

INTRODUCTION DE PHILIP JODIDIO

L'image et le symbole de « l'arbre de vie » courent à travers les religions, les philosophies et les mythologies depuis l'aube des temps, de l'Égypte ancienne à la Chine et à l'Amérique précolombienne. Lié au sol par ses racines et se projetant jusqu'au ciel, l'arbre est le modèle de l'architecture gothique. Sans lui, il n'y aurait pas eu de colonnes et ni peut-être de temple. Médiateur entre la terre et les cieux, l'arbre a toujours impressionné l'homme par sa taille, sa force et sa longévité qui semblent vouloir nous protéger, nous offrir un abri où nous reposer et rêver. De son sommet vertigineux, l'homme pouvait observer de haut le cadre de sa vie quotidienne, à la manière d'un oiseau en vol. C'était une rupture avec l'ordinaire de l'existence, un tremplin vers l'immortalité.

Que dans certaines cultures et sous certains climats les maisons ou cabanes dans les arbres aient été l'une des plus anciennes formes d'habitat nous est rappelé par les traditions architecturales encore actuelles de peuplades comme les Kombaï et les Korowaï, qui vivent dans les collines du pied des Monts Jayawijaya au sud-ouest d'Irian en Indonésie. Sans doute repoussés par des conflits tribaux ou divers fléaux, ces peuples construisent encore des maisons dans les arbres, à plus de quarante mètres de haut…

Si ce type d'habitat remonte à la nuit des temps et constitue certainement l'une des plus anciennes formes d'architecture, il est également présent dans l'histoire et l'art européens depuis l'époque des Romains. Dans son *Histoire naturelle*, Pline l'Ancien parle de l'empereur Caligula qui, dans un domaine situé à Velletri avait été impressionné par un banquet donné sur un plancher construit dans un platane et doté de bancs reposant sur les branches. On sait qu'en Europe, durant le Moyen Âge, des moines construisirent de petits ermitages dans des arbres à proximité de monastères, mais aussi que des maisons dans les arbres beaucoup plus spectaculaires existaient dans l'Italie de la Renaissance.

De Caligula au moine dominicain

Si Caligula a vécu de 12 à 41, plus de mille cinq cents ans plus tard les maisons dans les arbres faisaient toujours l'amusement des grands de l'Italie de la Renaissance. À la Villa di Castello en Toscane, Côme 1er de Médicis (1519-1574), premier duc de Toscane, avait fait dessiner par Niccolo Tribolo en 1538 un jardin dans lequel une petite maison dissimulée dans un chêne recouvert de lierre, offrait une salle à manger de plan carré. Dans son livre *Treehouses*, Anthony Aikman cite la description de ce jardin par Giorgio Vasari qui visita souvent le domaine :

« Il y avait des terrasses, des allées et des vergers et, dans un prairie à l'est de la villa, il planta une yeuse … recouverte d'un lierre si épais que l'on aurait dit un bosquet. Il construisit une coursive en escalier pour y accéder et fit aménager à son sommet une grande plate-forme entourée de sièges … avec des dossiers en verdure. Au centre se dressaient une table de marbre et un vase également en marbre bigarré alimenté par une canalisation d'eau qui jaillissait vers le ciel et s'évacuait par une autre conduite … Les conduites étaient tellement prises dans le lierre qu'elles étaient invisibles et le débit de l'eau était contrôlé par des robinets. Il est impossible de décrire la façon dont l'eau était transportée le long des branches de l'arbre pour arroser les gens en produisant de terribles sifflements. » Il est assez probable que Tribolo ait trouvé cette idée dans l'Hypnerotoromachia Poliphili, le célèbre récit de voyage poétique d'un moine dominicain, Francesco Colonna. Dans un paysage de fantaisie, le narrateur se trouve pris dans une charmille formée par l'entrelacs de branches d'arbres fruitiers : « Les branches et les rameaux étaient si artificiellement tordus et entremêlés que vous pouviez y monter sans être vu, et ne pas retrouver le chemin que vous aviez pris. »[1]

La fontaine du chêne

Le fils de Côme 1er, François de Médicis (1541–1587), commanda quant à lui une maison dans un arbre pour sa Villa de Pratolino (Vaglia, Toscane, 1569–1581), appelée la Fonte delle Rovere (La Fontaine du chêne), dotée d'escaliers en spirale conduisant à une plate-forme à 7, 5 mètres au-dessus du sol. Comme l'explique Aikman :

« Pour faire encore mieux que la maison dans l'arbre , Francesco avait encerclé l'yeuse de Pratolino non pas d'un mais de deux escaliers ! Ils montaient en spirale parallèlement l'un à l'autre de chaque côté de l'arbre. Rampes rythmées de marches plutôt que véritables escaliers, ils s'élevaient jusqu'à une plate-forme de huit mètres de diamètre où l'on trouvait une table de marbre, des sièges et des fontaines alimentées par des canalisations dissimulées le long des branches …. »

Montaigne (1533–1592) parle dans son *Journal de voyage en Italie* de Pratolino qu'il visita en 1580.

Le voyageur anglais Fynes Moryson (1566–1630) nous apprend également l'existence d'une maison dans un arbre équipée d'eau courante à Schaffouse en Suisse dans les années 1590 tandis que des tableaux de Pieter Breughel et d'autres peintres nous montrent des exemples de constructions flamandes similaires à la même période.

L'Angleterre est, bien sûr, l'un des principaux centres historiques de ces maisons dans les arbres avec, par exemple, celle de Cobham Hall dans le Kent ou encore celle, toujours existante, de Pitchford Hall près de Shrewsbury dans le Shropshire, citée pour la première fois en 1692. À la fin du XVIIᵉ siècle, cette mode très européenne et assez patricienne traversa l'Atlantique où l'on assista à la construction d'une maison dans un arbre dans les jardins du domaine de la Grange à Havertown en Pennsylvanie par le patriote américain John Ross.[2]

Le Robinson suisse chez Walt Disney

Si certains de ces exemples historiques présentent un aspect presque «légendaire», les maisons dans les arbres entrent au XIXᵉ siècle dans une nouvelle phase où la fiction devient réalité. En 1845, un cabaret en forme de maisonnettes dans les arbres reliées entre elles appelé Le Grand Robinson ouvrit ses portes au Plessis-Piquet près de Paris. À l'apogée de son succès, il n'accueillait pas moins de 200 tables. Son nom venait du titre d'un roman de 1812 *Le Robinson suisse* écrit par le pasteur helvète Johann David Wyss, lui-même emprunté au célèbre ouvrage de Daniel Defoe, *Robinson Crusoe* datant de 1712. En 1909, la commune du Plessis-Riquet prit le nom de Plessis-Robinson, hommage surprenant à deux livres célèbres et à un cabaret perché dans les arbres.

L'histoire de la maison dans un arbre de la famille suisse des Robinson a connu une métamorphose étonnante. À la suite d'un film réalisé d'après ce livre en 1960 par Walt Disney, La Maison dans l'arbre des Robinson suisses est devenue une attraction des parcs Disney dans le monde entier. Réalisée de façons à ressembler à un arbre véritable, comme dans le film, cette version de 18 mètres de haut est en acier, béton et stuc. Ornée de 1400 branches, 300 000 feuilles en polyéthylène et d'un peu de vraie mousse espagnole, cette étrange structure témoigne de la puissance populaire du mythe des maisons dans les arbres. Revenant sur l'origine de la signification symbolique de l'arbre, le parc à thème de Disney, «Le Royaume des animaux» comporte lui aussi un «arbre de vie» inspiré de l'attraction des Robinson suisses.

La gentille Julia dans son séquoia

L'histoire des maisons dans les arbres présentées dans cet ouvrage dépasse ainsi l'histoire connue. Beaucoup d'idées qui ont inspiré les premières cabanes de ce type sont encore très présentes dans les réalisations contemporaines, du désir d'isolement à la proximité de la nature ou à la sensation vertigineuse de se retrouver perché loin du sol. La montée en puissance de l'intérêt pour un habitat et une architecture écologiquement responsables ou durables en Europe et aux États-Unis, en particulier depuis les années 1990, a certainement contribué à la multiplication du nombre d'entreprises spécialisées dans la conception et la construction de maisons dans les arbres. Elle reflète le développement important et soutenu de l'intérêt du public pour toutes sortes de maisons dans les arbres, de la simple plate-forme à la retraite sophistiquée équipée d'écrans plasma et d'alarmes anti-intrusion. L'arbre-image-de-la-vie qui reste l'un des plus puissants symboles de la nature et de sa défense, parfois repris dans la rhétorique des écologistes radicaux, s'est également incarné dans une certaine vision de maison dans l'arbre. L'environnementaliste américaine Julia «Papillon» Hill a créé des plates-formes de trois mètres carrés à 60 mètres du sol dans un séquoia géant californien vieux de 1500 ans et y a vécu 738 jours entre 1997 et 1999 pour empêcher des bûcherons de l'abattre. Cette action est devenue un des symboles les plus forts de l'activisme écologique aux États-Unis et a même été célébré dans un certain nombre de chansons populaires.

Se détendre, rêver le jour...

Ce qui est nouveau depuis dix ou quinze ans est l'apparition d'un certain nombre de créateurs compétents d'excellente formation qui ont fait de ce type de maison leur spécialité. L'un d'entre eux est un ancien ébéniste, Andreas Wenning, né en 1965 en Allemagne. Basé à Brême, il a construits plusieurs maisons dans les arbres d'esprit très contemporain, dont certaines sont publiées dans cet ouvrage. Le texte d'introduction que Wenning a rédigé pour son site web résume le sentiment d'excitation et de découverte que son œuvre et celle de ses confrères suscitent : « Une maison dans l'arbre ! Une promesse d'aventure pour les gosses, de retraite pour les adultes, de cachette romantique au plus proche de la nature. Ces petites habitations très particulières installées si haut dans les arbres enflamment notre imagination et interpellent notre curiosité en nous rappelant des souvenirs d'enfance et, avec eux, le désir de grimper toujours plus haut et de pénétrer dans un monde magique perdu tout là-haut dans les feuillages, pour se ré-enchanter, pour observer la nature sous différentes perspectives, ses bruits de jour et de nuit au fil des saisons, pour jouer tout là-haut, pour travailler sans être dérangé, se détendre, rêvasser ... » Les réalisations de Wenning appliquent d'authentiques principes de design et d'architecture à cette typologie particulière, mais ses projets non réalisés s'orientent plutôt vers des formes d'avant-garde. Ses maisons appelées Serpent lové, Boucle et Cône font appel bien sûr à sa connaissance des arbres mais restent étonnamment proches de ce qui se fait dans les constructions au sol. En dépit des gadgets et de diverses formes de modernité introduites dans d'autres projets de ce type à travers le monde, Wenning s'est positionné comme une sorte de leader dans le domaine de la maison dans l'arbre contemporaine.

Un pont, un tipi et un voilier

Des approches contemporaines de conception adaptées aux structures des maisons suspendues sont également à la base de la réflexion du jeune designer américain Dustin Feider (O2 Treehouse) qui utilise des matériaux comme l'HDPE (bouteilles plastique recyclées) et le système des structures géodésiques de Buckminster Fuller, soit la forme la plus économique en terme de matériaux pour créer un volume donné (page 148). Son projet de Maison dans l'arbre Blum (Hollywood, Californie, 2009) a la forme d'un pont tandis que son Tree Pi (Santa Monica, Californie, 2008) rappelle le type tout aussi simple du tipi. Feider, qui n'a pas vingt-cinq ans, représente une nouvelle génération de constructeurs de cabanes dans les arbres, qui possède une bonne connaissance des formes et de leur dynamique sans craindre les expérimentations ni de mettre en pratique les leçons de l'architecture contemporaine. En dehors des sphères triangulées des structures géodésiques, un autre designer américain, Tom Chudleigh, s'est inspiré de l'univers de la construction navale pour imaginer ses Free Spirit Spheres (Qualicum Beach, Colombie britanniques, Canada, page 134) suspendues dans les airs. Même les attaches de ses sphères renvoient à l'ingénierie navale, modèle éventuellement adapté à un objet qui se balance dans le vent mais référence néanmoins inattendue.

Châteaux aériens de contes de fées

En réalité, beaucoup si ce n'est la plupart des concepteurs de maisons dans les arbres restent loin de l'image de modernité qu'Andreas Wenning ou Dustin Feider défendent aujourd'hui. C'est le cas des constructions souvent à toit de chaume ou de shingles de la firme britannique Blue Forest. Leur High-Tech Hideaway (Athènes, Grèce, 2004) associe un toit de chaume à des éléments contemporains comme un circuit de surveillance vidéo et un écran de télévision plat. Confortablement aménagée, cette maison semble un compromis entre la modernité et un aspect qui évoque davantage la forêt de Sherwood que la Silicon Valley. Le projet de Blue Forest pour une salle à manger dans les arbres (Leatherhead, Surrey, G.-B.) pourrait même rappeler les légendaires maisons dans les arbres anglaises ou même celles des Médicis. Imaginez un dîner élégant pour des gens célèbres ou non ? Tout rêve devient réalisable.

Deux entreprises françaises ont choisi une approche différente mais très ambitieuse. La première, Dans mon arbre, est basée à Grenoble. Sous la direction de Frank Coursier, elle s'attache à concevoir à travers ses « cabanes » des projets respectueux de l'arbre qui les accueille. Ses réalisations ne sont pas immédiatement identifiables car elle pratique des styles très différents. Le projet pour Langeais (La Cabane du château de Langeais, Parc de l'an mil, château de Langeais, France, 2008, page 216) est un assemblage de formes et de couleurs que ne répudieraient pas nombre d'architectes contemporains. Collaborant avec le designer Renaud Morel, Dans mon arbre a franchi plusieurs pas pour se rapprocher de créations architecturales « terrestres» d'assez haut niveau. La Cabane de Kallerput (Eindhoven, Pays-Bas, 2010, page 196) ne totalise pas moins de 165 mètres carrés, beaucoup plus donc que la norme habituelle pour ce type d'habitat. Le Village aérien (2009, page 40) non encore construit, mis au point avec Benoît Fray, se compose d'une série de chambres de type hôtel à ossature autoportante en mélèze de 33 mètres carrés. À l'autre extrémité du spectre, on trouve une cabane-bateau (Meudon, près de Paris, 2009), projet de 12 000 euros réalisé pour des enfants dans un mélèze. Cette maison ne se prétend pas à l'avant-garde de l'architecture, mais atteint le but parfaitement louable de faire plaisir à des enfants, ce qui est l'un des principaux objectifs de la plupart des réalisations présentées dans ce livre.

Une cabane pour aimer

Les projets de La Cabane perchée, agence du Sud de la France créée en 2000 par Alain Laurens, sont des propositions intelligentes et très sophistiquées qui restent néanmoins dans un registre esthétique de la maison dans l'arbre classique. Cachées dans le feuillage, souvent accessibles par de vertigineux escaliers en spirale, ces cabanes réalisées avec l'aide du maître-charpentier Ghislain André sont principalement destinées aux adultes «pour observer lire ou écrire, écouter de la musique, se sentir bien, rêver, être seul de temps en temps, aimer parfois », comme l'écrit Laurens. Il fait cependant remarquer que même si ces maisons sont destinées à des adultes, elle correspondent souvent à la matérialisation de rêves d'enfants, ceux du client, mais aussi ceux de leur concepteur et de leurs constructeurs. Ce travail, généralement accompagné de séduisantes aquarelles peintes par Daniel Dufour, a été largement reproduit dans des livres publiés par les dirigeants de l'agence. La Cabane perchée a construit plus de 220 maisons dans les arbres en Europe, souvent pour de prestigieux clients, ce qui en fait l'une des équipes spécialisées les plus performantes dans ce domaine.

Malgré ce grand succès, la Cabane perchée, comme la plupart de ses consœurs, s'appuie en grande partie sur le travail d'artisans, à l'opposé d'une approche industrielle que des gens comme Guislain André évitent généralement. Concrètement, chaque cabane et chaque arbre tendent à être uniques et c'est la raison pour laquelle ce type d'architecture remet en question un certain nombre des présupposés sur lesquels reposent d'autres types de constructions. Ces maisons ont souvent besoin de permis de construire strictement contrôlés, dépendant du lieu où elles sont érigées et relèvent donc du domaine de l'architecture, même si beaucoup de leurs concepteurs et constructeurs ne possèdent pas de diplôme d'ingénieur ou d'architecte. Cette profession compte probablement plus de menuisiers et d'arboristes que d'architectes au sens traditionnel du terme.

Planter la graine

En dehors d'entreprises de tailles diverses comme Blue Forest ou La Cabane perchée, l'univers de la conception et de la construction des maisons dans les arbres est peuplé d'un certain nombre de fortes personnalités, hommes pour la plupart, qui n'ont pas reçu de formation d'architecte mais sont motivées par une puissante envie de faire revivre un peu du monde imaginaire de leur enfance. Ce désir rencontre souvent celui de leurs clients. L'un de ces designers les plus connus aux États-Unis est Pete Nelson qui se présente ainsi sur son site web : «Très tôt, j'ai été fasciné par une activité dont je me sentais capable, le travail du bois. Jeune garçon, j'ai construit quelques cabanes dans des arbres avec mon père et des amis et conçu mon premier grand projet dans ce domaine alors que j'étais encore au collège. Il ne fut jamais réalisé mais la petite graine de la maison dans l'arbre était plantée.» Nelson n'a pas seulement conçu et construit de nombreuses cabanes perchées mais enseigne également leurs méthodes de construction et les utilise même pour faciliter le contact de personnes handicapées avec la nature. Sa notoriété relative est due pour une bonne part à la publication de plusieurs ouvrages. Il suffit d'ailleurs de chercher pour s'apercevoir que le nombre des livres sur le sujet s'est récemment multiplié, ce qui montre bien que ces constructions entre rêve et réalité ont su toucher une corde sensible au sein du grand public.

Roderick Wolgamott Romero, né en 1965 à Seattle, est un autre acteur intéressant de ce domaine. Depuis la fin des années 1990, il a construit des maisons suspendues pour des célébrités comme le chanteur Sting, les acteurs Val Kilmer et Julianne Moore ou la styliste de mode Donna Karan. Il défend une approche très basique et utilise presque uniquement des matériaux récupérés ou recyclés. Il fait également appel à des artisans locaux pour l'aider sur ses projets qui tendent à se fondre agréablement dans leur environnement. Du fait de ses préoccupations écologiques, de la façon dont il utilise les matériaux, mais aussi de sa conception de son travail, ses maisons semblent naturellement posées dans les arbres, rappelant parfois autant un abri, voire un nid, qu'une «vraie» maison. On peut noter dans son travail un certain nombre de différences entre les pratiques de l'architecture contemporaine et celles de la conception de maisons dans les arbres, sans qu'elles ne s'excluent. Les réalisations de Romero apportent un élément de fantaisie et une image résolument «verte» qui dépasse la rhétorique écologique de la plupart des architectes. Par l'utilisation de matériaux de récupération, principalement le bois, et une approche délibérément *low-tech* de la construction, ces structures vont plus loin encore dans leur inspiration que les tables dans le ciel imaginées par les Médicis. C'est le refuge d'un chasseur peut-être, mais d'un chasseur aimable qui observe surtout la nature, un abri, au sens physique ou métaphysique, où pouvoir se retirer du monde.

Ma compagne est la vie même

Sur l'autre rive du Pacifique, au Japon cette fois, le designer Takashi Kobayashi s'est forgé une réputation internationale à travers un style ludique et participatif qui a donné naissance à quelques spectaculaires cabanes perchées. «Parfois je me demande ce que je serais aujourd'hui si, il y a seize ans, je n'avais pas emménagé dans un petit appartement d'un immeuble en bois d'une ruelle de Harajuku», écrit-il sur son site web. «Je pense au cèdre de l'Himalaya que j'y ai trouvé et au tour fondamentalement différent que ma vie aurait certainement pris et je ne peux m'empêcher de sentir ici la présence de quelque puissance invisible. Appelez cela le destin, si vous voulez. Qu'est-ce qu'ont donc ces maisons dans les arbres pour avoir su capter l'imagination d'un paresseux comme moi, qui n'avait jamais pu me consacrer à la moindre cause ni finir quoi que ce soit que j'avais commencé? Qu'est-ce qui nous attire dans ces maisons perchées? J'en suis venu à penser que la réponse n'était pas sans rapport avec la vitalité même des arbres. Avec la vie éternelle.» Cette description de motivations personnelles penche vers une communion spirituelle avec les arbres et la nature et fait ressortir certaines raisons qui expliquent pourquoi la conception, la construction et l'utilisation de maisons dans les arbres est devenue un phénomène aussi répandu au cours des dernières années. «La construction de maisons dans les arbres m'a fait découvrir des forêts et des régions boisées dans tout le Japon et même dans le monde», continue Kobayashi, «et partout où je suis allé, j'ai senti dans ces être vivants que sont les arbres, parfois les plus grands et les plus vieux du monde, la même lumière mystérieuse que j'ai essayé de maintenir allumée en moi depuis tant d'années, que rien ne peut ternir et qui ne semble jamais prête à disparaître. Ce confort, ce sens du calme, est quelque chose que j'aimerais partager avec le plus grand nombre de gens possible. C'est en pensant à cela que je poursuivrai cette expérience si unique qu'est la création d'une maison dans un arbre, tout en continuant mon dialogue personnel avec son hôte. Parce que ma compagne est la vie même. Et aussi longtemps qu'existeront des arbres encore non découverts...»

Une maison de thé trop haute

Dans une approche assez différente de la communion avec la nature revendiquée par Takashi Kobayashi, un certain nombre d'architectes contemporains, plus connus pour leurs constructions au sol que dans les arbres, ont pris plaisir à imaginer des maisons dans les arbres. Le plus proche de la réflexion de Kobayashi – pas seulement parce qu'il est lui aussi japonais –, est Terunobu Fujimori. Né en 1946, Fujimori, professeur à l'Institut des sciences industrielles de l'Université de Tokyo, a commencé à pratiquer l'architecture à une date assez tardive, par rapport à la coutume, mais a vite rejoint les rangs des architectes japonais contemporains les plus influents et les plus publiés. Il joue à la fois sur les références aux traditions architecturales japonaises et sur l'inévitable rapport à la nature qu'elles impliquent. Il a construit plusieurs maisons de thé au Japon, à partir de la longue réflexion historique sur ces constructions, et s'est aventuré à Taïwan où ce type architectural s'est un peu libéré de la rigueur des règles habituelles. Son Nid à thé d'Irisenteî (Beipu, Taïwan, 2010, page 184) n'est certainement pas une maison de thé au sens classique du terme mais est positionné très loin du sol au sommet d'un tronc de bambou géant. La Takasugi-an ou «Maison de thé trop haute» (Chino, Nagano, Japon, 2004, page 304) est petite mais utilise un vocabulaire qui fait penser aux maisons

Mais pourquoi donc les maisons dans les arbres ne pourraient-elles franchir ce fossé?

Aluminium et miroir

L'une des réalisations les plus surprenantes publiées dans cet ouvrage est peut-être le Tree Hotel construit à Harads en Suède (2008, page 238) par les talentueux architectes Bolle Tham (né en 1970) et Martin Videgård (né en 1968). Leur agence, Tham & Videgård a créé une étonnante «chambre» d'hôtel parée d'aluminium léger qui n'est évidemment pas le matériau favori des créateurs de ce type de maisons. L'intérieur doublé de contreplaqué offre tout le confort moderne, dont une kitchenette et un lit double. Si l'idée de cube en aluminium poli miroir a déjà été utilisée par des architectes dans le passé, il fallait une certaine imagination pour imaginer d'en percher un dans un arbre. Cette chambre offre à ses occupants une vue à 360° sur la forêt environnante et rompt avec les conceptions stéréotypées que l'on pourrait avoir d'un projet moderne. Sous certains angles, elle semble tout simplement disparaître dans son cadre, ce qui lui assure une certaine qualité écologique même si les matériaux modernes utilisés, n'ont rien à voir avec les planches sciées à la main préférées par d'autres constructeurs. Installer le confort moderne dans un arbre sous une forme aussi pure requiert à l'évidence un vrai travail d'architecte et range cet hôtel dans les arbres dans une catégorie à part de celle de beaucoup d'autres maisons dans les arbres.

Une autre réalisation résolument contemporaine est le restaurant de la Cabane jaune dans l'arbre (Warkworth, Nouvelle-Zélande, 2008, page 338) conçue par les architectes d'Auckland, Pacific Environments. Ce restaurant de 44 mètres carrés en forme de coquillage est installé à 10 mètres au-dessus du sol. Il peut recevoir 18 personnes y compris le personnel. La cuisine et les toilettes sont au sol et on accède à la «salle» par une passerelle suspendue de 60 mètres de long. «C'est la maison dans un arbre dont nous avons tous rêvé quand nous étions enfants mais ne pouvions réaliser qu'une fois devenus adultes», explique Peter Eising, son auteur, rappelant une thématique récurrente. Ici, l'intervention d'architectes de talent a permis de créer un vrai restaurant et de donner à ce projet des ambitions qui n'auraient pu être atteintes sans vraie formation, sans conception moderne et sans méthodes de construction actuelles. Là encore, même si cette maison échappe au manque de sophistication volontaire de la plupart des maisons dans les arbres, l'intervention d'architectes praticiens dans la canopée ouvre de nouveaux horizons. Ses utilisateurs retrouvent néanmoins la plupart des sensations que ceux qui grimpent dans une cabane de bois perchée, de l'excitation de l'observation de la nature sous un angle nouveau au vertige provoqué par la hauteur des arbres choisis comme support.

Lorsque la terre tremblera

En Nouvelle-Zélande également, l'Hapuku Lodge (Kaikoura, Ile du Sud, page 160) est gérée par la famille Wilson qui compte plusieurs architectes en son sein. À travers son agence, Wilson Architects, cette famille a créé sur sa propriété des maisons perchées dans des manukas, une essence locale. Visiblement conçues par des architectes, elles ne sont pas vraiment des maisons dans les arbres au sens habituel puisqu'elles s'appuient en fait sur des poutrelles en acier. La raison en est de mieux résister aux tremblements de terre mais aussi d'offrir des espaces plus adaptés au confort moderne que les cabanes en bois

japonaises traditionnelles. Offrant une vue cadrée sur la ville dans laquelle l'architecte a grandi, cette construction possède un but mieux défini que la plupart des maisons dans les arbres et manifeste un sens de l'humour qui n'est pas toujours le point fort des concepteurs de «maisons dans les arbres de luxe» vues dans d'autres pays. Les créations de Fujimori présentent des aspects très particuliers aussi bien dans leur construction que dans leur fonction, qui vont au-delà de ce que l'on trouve habituellement dans les réalisations de praticiens dont la culture architecturale et la culture tout court sont moins sophistiquées. En d'autres termes, les maisons dans les arbres de Terunobu Fujimori se situent à un niveau très différent. Il partage avec Kobayashi un même intérêt pour la nature, bien que sans doute plus distant et plus sublimé, et les deux hommes entretiennent à l'évidence un rapport étroit avec la culture de leur pays.

Beaucoup moins connu que Fujimori, Lukasz Kos est né à Starachowice en Pologne en 1978. Il a étudié le design environnemental à l'Université du Manitoba au Canada (2000), obtenu un M.A. en Pologne et un M. Arch. à Toronto en 2006. Sa 4Tree House (Walker's Point, lac Muskoka, Ontario, Canada, 2003, page 34) est une construction de trois niveaux qui se développe parmi quatre arbres. Ce projet s'éloigne radicalement du conte de fées au profit de l'architecture contemporaine.

perchées habituelles. Les Wilson sont visiblement très conscients des conséquences que leurs actions pourraient avoir sur la nature mais savent tirer profit non seulement des sensations produites par leur site naturel magnifique mais aussi par les hauteurs vertigineuses de leurs maisons, habituellement plutôt le fait de tours d'observation ou de nids d'oiseaux. L'adaptation de la forme et du concept de la maison dans l'arbre à un type architectural plus solidement ancré dans le sol est aussi un signe de l'emprise de ce genre de maison sur l'imagination et même les corps. Se retrouver au sommet d'un arbre correspond certainement à un désir de fuite et de pouvoirs sur la nature qui échappent habituellement aux simples humains. Un peu comme le désir de voler dans les airs.

_____ Et maintenant, le rétro-futur

Bien que les maisons dans les arbres ne soient peut-être pas la plus évidente des formes d'expression artistique contemporaine, certains artistes n'en ont pas moins été tentés part le genre. Deux exemples de ces démarches sont présentés dans ce livre, le premier nourri de contre-culture américaine et l'autre perché au sommet d'un arbre en Suède. La Steampunk Tree House (actuellement installée à Milton, Delaware, États-Unis, 2007, page 298) est l'œuvre d'un artiste nommé Sean Orlando and the Five Ton Crane Arts Group. Son propriétaire actuel parle de « sculpture rétrofuturiste décalée » créée pour le Burning Man Festival 2007 à Black Rock City dans le Nevada. Il ne s'agit pas vraiment d'une maison dans l'arbre au sens propre puisqu'elle a été construite à l'aide de pas moins de huit tonnes de matériaux recyclés et de récupération. Le Burning Man est un festi-

val d'une semaine, présenté par ses organisateurs comme « une expérience de vie communautaire, d'auto-expression et d'autosuffisance radicales ». 50 000 personnes environ ont participé à son édition 2010. Sean Orlando explique que la « Steampunk Tree House a été réalisée pour explorer les relations entre notre monde naturel en changement rapide et la tendance humaine persistante à s'y connecter. C'est notre seconde nature ». Bien qu'elle ait pris la forme d'un arbre, cette maison est une sculpture et le fait qu'elle utilise plus le métal et autres matériaux de récupération que le bois répond au commentaire d'Orlando sur la « tendance humaine persistante » à se connecter avec la nature. Même si elle ne possède pas de racines, cette maison incarne de multiples façons les mêmes motivations qui ont conduit tant d'autres à s'emparer des arbres.

Autre artiste travaillant hors des sentiers battus, le Suédois Mikael Grenberg a construit une vraie maison dans un arbre. C'est en 1999 qu'il a eu la curieuse idée d'envoyer une petite maison rouge et blanche sur la lune après avoir entendu parler des plans de lancement d'un nouveau satellite appelé SMART-1 par l'Agence spatiale nationale suédoise. Imaginant qu'une petite maison inspirée de l'architecture résidentielle traditionnelle suédoise pourrait « symboliser la foi des gens dans la capacité au changement », il créa la Fondation de la maison sur la lune pour l'humanité, qui se proposait de décerner un prix annuel « à toute personne, organisation ou entreprise qui pouvait faire de la terre un endroit meilleur ». Ce projet n'a existé que dans l'imagination de l'artiste qui a cependant réellement conçu une maison capable d'être déposée sur la lune par un engin lunaire sans pilote. Dans ce contexte, il a également créé l'Utter Inn, un très petit hôtel sous-marin auquel on accède via une maisonnette rouge et blanche flottant sur le lac Mälaren près de sa ville natale de Västerås. Dans la même veine, le Hackspett Tree House Hotel, également situé à Västerås domine le sol de 13 mètres. C'est une fois encore une petite maison rouge et blanche qui fait ainsi lien avec l'obsession permanente de cet artiste pour ce symbole très suédois de l'idée d'espoir, ou peut-être d'excentricité, selon les points de vue. L'artiste français Jean-Pierre Raynaud a longtemps cherché à placer ses pots de fleurs surdimensionnés dans des lieux très variés, de la Cité interdite à Pékin à des emplacements souterrains ou dans l'espace. Son processus de pensée était similaire à celui de Genberg, utiliser un objet ordinaire comme symbole d'espoir et de régénération. L'hôtel de la maison dans l'arbre du pic-vert est en soi un lieu amusant où passer la nuit, mais dans le contexte de l'œuvre de Mikael Genberg et de son processus de pensée, il prend une dimension plus vaste que celles dont les concepteurs de cabanes dans les arbres n'ont jamais rêvé.

_____ Deux nuits, deux rêves

Aujourd'hui, l'une des occasions les plus courantes de vivre sa passion pour les arbres est de descendre dans l'un de ses hôtels perchés qui offrent un degré plus ou moins élevé de confort. Si ce ne sont pas toujours les exemples les plus sophistiqués et les plus intéressants de ce type de structure au plan architectural, ils sont en revanche consacrés à un usage concret, pratique et se devaient de figurer dans cet ouvrage. Étant donné l'intérêt toujours croissant pour les vacances écologiques et la demande des vacanciers pour une proximité réelle avec la nature, des hôtels dans les arbres se sont développés sur tous les continents, même si l'Europe et l'Afrique semblent mener le mouvement.

En France, le Natura Cabana propose un certain nombre de chambres de ce genre sur les terres du château Malleret dans le Médoc, en Aquitaine. Ce projet répond à l'aventure personnelle de sa responsable, Prune Gouet, ancienne spécialiste des ventes, qui a créé cinq maisons dans les arbres sans l'assistance d'architectes, juste accompagnée d'un constructeur et aidée de son sens des formes et de sa connaissance des attentes de ses clients potentiels. L'association d'une exploitation viticole qui produit des vins de qualité, de cet hôtel et de son cadre naturel fait d'un séjour aux Natura Cabana une expérience rare. La proposition commerciale « Deux nuits, deux rêves » combine une nuit dans les arbres et une nuit au château Malleret. Natura Cabana a reçu quelques subventions du département de la Gironde et insiste fortement sur l'identité écologique du projet et la nature durable de ces installations dans les arbres. L'hôtel est membre d'une organisation appelée Bio-organic Holidays.[3]

Les Nids, installés au Locle dans le canton de Neuchâtel en Suisse, est un autre projet européen de dimensions similaires. Le couple qui le gère propose un grand nombre d'activités dans la région, du football au ski. Bien que d'apparence assez rustique, Les Nids offrent de petits « luxes » comme une cuisinette, une douche et des toilettes ce qui n'est pas si courant dans ce type d'habitat. Comme pour Natura Cabana, l'idée est ici la proximité avec la nature ou peut-être la rupture avec le monde plus « civilisé » des grandes villes et de la vie moderne. Comme dans le Médoc, le tourisme occupe une place importante dans la présentation des Nids sur Internet.

En sympathie avec la nature, en lien avec elle

L'architecte américain David Greenberg précise qu'il a étudié l'architecture et l'urbanisme avant d'essayer « de reconstruire Los Angeles après les émeutes du début des années 1990 ». Il fait partie d'une génération qui, comme celle des années 1960, a voulu repartir de zéro et changer le monde à sa façon. Il admet s'être inspiré des expérimentations menées à Hawaï autour des maisons dans les arbres des années 1970 et, maintenant à son compte, en construit à Hawaï et, de façon plus surprenante, en Chine. Il a conçu la Maison dans l'arbre de la Grande plage dans le ciel (page 64), la Maison dans l'arbre de Guanyin et l'Hôtel dans les arbres Hawaiian Hale près du parc à thème bouddhiste et écologique de 2000 hectares de Sanya Nanshan sur l'île de Hainan (Chine, 2000). Dans ces constructions et celle de Hawaï, Greenberg précise que son intérêt porte sur « la création d'une architecture en sympathie avec la nature et en lien avec elle, en particulier sous des climats tropicaux ». Là encore, les préoccupations écologiques et la tentative de se rapprocher de la nature motivent les efforts. On observe dans ses réalisations un style volontairement pittoresque qui fait certainement référence à la réalisation de rêves d'enfants ou de rêveries d'adolescents ou d'adultes voire la fuite et le retour à une vie plus « authentique » que celle menée dans les grandes villes des États-Unis ou de Chine. La Maison dans l'arbre de la canopée (page 90) par Ikaterra, près de Puerto Maldonado au Pérou est une sorte de solution médiane entre l'écologie et le tourisme. Située dans la Reserva Amazonica, réserve écologique privée de 104 kilomètres carrés en pleine forêt pluviale amazonienne près du parc national de Tambopata, le projet regroupe un gîte au sol et des structures qui se développent dans la canopée à une hauteur de 30 à 60 mètres. Un réseau de passerelles, de plates-formes et de tours offre aux visiteurs des vues privilégiées sur l'écosystème. La diversité biologique et végétale du lieu est exception-

nelle et les visiteurs étrangers affluent dans ces maisons suspendues. La description figurant sur le site Internet montre clairement que le confort va de pair avec la découverte écologique : « Pour faire la découverte la plus exclusive et la plus mémorable de la forêt pluviale, la Canopy Tree House offre un isolement absolu parmi les splendeurs du sud-est de l'Amazonie péruvienne. Construite sur une plate-forme privée le long de la célèbre Passerelle de la canopée à quelque 27 mètres au-dessus du niveau d'une végétation luxuriante, l'Inkaterra Canopy Tree House offre des services sans équivalents et un séjour dans la jungle de qualité incomparable. De ce remarquable point de vue en suspension dans la canopée, les hôtes pourront observer toutes sortes d'espèces d'animaux sauvages qui ne sont généralement pas visibles du sol et écouter les étonnants bruits de la jungle tout en se détendant au Bar de la canopée. Plus tard, ils pourront aussi se plonger dans l'atmosphère de la forêt et prendre un repas léger en contemplant les étoiles avant de se promener dans l'univers nocturne, secret et fascinant du sommet des grands arbres. »[4]

Pavillon de chasse visuelle

C'est une approche différente de la vie sauvage que pratique la réserve de chasse privée de Lion Sands (Mpumalanga, Afrique du Sud) dont les hôtes peuvent séjourner dans la quasi légendaire Chalkley Tree House (page 98) construite sur un site où Guy Aubrey Chalkley installa son campement pour se protéger des prédateurs dans les années 1930. Il créa la même année le Lion Sands dans la Sabi Sand Game Reserve, à l'intérieur du parc national Kruger. Ses concepteurs parlent de « chambre dans la brousse » et c'est en fait davantage une plate-forme qu'une maison dans un arbre au sens propre. Elle est construite autour d'un chigomier, ou arbre de fer, vieux de 500 ans et ne peut accueillir plus de deux personnes à la fois, qui ont ainsi la chance de voir la faune sauvage se déplacer en liberté dans cette réserve sans barrières. Cette proximité de la nature combine le confort d'un vrai lit à la froide réalité de la vie naturelle africaine. C'est la maison dans les arbres, refuge contre les bêtes sauvages, qui a moins à voir avec l'attirance pour le vertige de l'altitude et la fuite des contraintes terrestres qu'à l'observation perchée de créatures de la nature en voie de disparition rapide et se livrant à leur occupation vitale, la chasse.

Les amoureux des animaux trouveront également leur bonheur dans le Logis de la maison dans l'arbre de Pezula à Hoedspruit, province du Limpopo, également en Afrique du Sud. Il s'agit de constructions sur pilotis implantées entre des arbres qui offrent divers agréments dont une salle de bains avec jacuzzi. N'importe laquelle de ces constructions aurait pu être édifiée au sol, mais perchées dans les arbres, elles prennent un air beaucoup plus exotique et permettent de voir les animaux en liberté. La maison dans l'arbre du voyage de noces (Honeymoon Tree house) de Pezulu propose un lit de grandes dimensions et une baignoire en creux avec vue sur une mare où des girafes et des zèbres viennent boire.

Comme les Médicis

La séduction exercée par ce type de structures ne fait aucun doute, mais on constate une tendance mondiale à en « domestiquer » l'idée et à y installer le confort d'une vraie maison. Une baignoire en creux, un écran de télévision ultraplat et la signature de grands architectes font maintenant partie de la gamme des propositions. Beaucoup de constructions actuelles ressemblent curieusement à des maisons normales, peut-être un peu plus petites et qui auraient pu être aussi bien installées au sol. Certains signes montrent que le succès de l'idée de maisons dans les arbres s'éloigne du modèle classique du refuge rêvé où l'on se protège du monde « réel », même s'il perdure encore. Quelques siècles plus tôt cependant, les Médicis avaient déjà installé des tables de marbre et de riches buffets dans leurs maisons perchées de Castello et de Pratolino. La séduction qu'exercent ces structures tient peu être à leur incongruité et au fait que l'homme n'est pas vraiment fait pour vivre dans les arbres. La solidité, la stabilité du sol est une de nos sensations les plus fondamentales et les plus nécessaires, et une cabane dans un arbre supprime cette certitude rassurante au profit d'un léger balancement et de la crainte de tomber. De même que les pièces de Shakespeare mettent en scène des personnages menés par le destin dans un bois où les faux-semblants disparaissent tandis que se révèle une autre réalité, les maisons dans les arbres offrent un abri pour dormir et peut-être rêver. Certaines sont édifiées dans des chênes solitaires près d'une grande demeure, mais d'autres sont en pleine forêt, comme le bien nommé Temple de la lune bleue présenté dans cet ouvrage (Issaquah, État de Washington, 2006, page 316).

La maison dans l'arbre nous raconte une histoire aussi ancienne que celle de l'architecture ou peut-être que celle des abris construits par l'homme, des abris pour se protéger, s'échapper et, de nos jours, retrouver la paix et la proximité de la nature dans un monde qui dénie de plus en plus ce qui faisait partie de notre existence même. La maison dans l'arbre prend des airs de luxe, comme les chalets des Alpes qui sont devenus des hôtels cinq étoiles au lieu de rester les humbles refuges de bois brut qu'ils étaient. Aujourd'hui, on trouve dans les maisons perchées l'eau chaude courante et l'Internet. Même si elles n'ont plus guère de liens avec leurs ancêtres, les cabanes actuelles conservent cependant une simplicité réelle et nous proposent une sorte de nouvelle Arcadie. D'autres constructions réunissent le meilleur de deux opposés : l'innocence de la nature d'avant la chute et le confort du grand écran.

Ces tours qui se perdent dans les nues …

Dans l'œuvre du peintre français Nicolas Poussin, deux tableaux représentent des bergers vêtus à l'Antique se tenant devant un tombeau sur lequel sont gravés les mots *Et in Arcadia ego*, que l'on a traduit par « Et moi aussi, j'ai vécu en Arcadie ». Le mythe de l'Arcadie, une région de la Grèce antique, est celui d'une vie en harmonie avec la nature, une vie idéalisée, le contraire du « progrès » moderne. La maison dans l'arbre serait ainsi beaucoup plus le défi de grimper ou de construire – et de chuter – et d'échapper à quelque chose et d'y revenir. Elle symboliserait la fuite devant les pressions de la vie moderne et le retour à une existence plus simple dans laquelle la dépendance de la nature est un fait. Ne voir que l'arbre dans ce rêve de châteaux dans les feuillages est un peu comme ne voir que l'arbre qui cache la forêt. Bien qu'elle se présente sous de multiples variantes, la maison dans les arbres nous parle en fait de la forêt, le lieu de nos origines. Souvent éphémères et incertaines, ces maisons sont pour certains les « tours qui se perdent dans les nues, les palais somptueux » dont parle Prospero dans *La Tempête* de Shakespeare (Acte IV, scène 1) :

« Maintenant voilà nos divertissements finis ; nos acteurs, comme je vous l'ai dit d'avance, étaient tous des esprits ; ils se sont fondus en air, en air subtil ; et, pareils à l'édifice sans base de cette vision, se dissou-

dront aussi les tours qui se perdent dans les nues, les palais somptueux, les temples solennels, notre vaste globe, oui, notre globe lui-même, et tout ce qu'il reçoit de la succession des temps ; et comme s'est évanoui cet appareil mensonger, ils se dissoudront, sans même laisser derrière eux la trace que laisse le nuage emporté par le vent. Nous sommes faits de la vaine substance dont se forment les songes, et notre chétive vie est environnée d'un sommeil ».

Les maisons dans les arbres qui illustrent cette introduction sont celles des Korowai, un peuple de l'Irian Jaya (Nouvelle-Guinée, Indonésie). Elles ont été photographiées par Harald Melcher, photographe et explorateur allemand.

1 Anthony Aikman, *Treehouses*, Robert Hale, Londres, 1988.
2 Anthony Aikman, *Treehouses*, Robert Hale, Londres, 1988
3 http://www.bio-organic-holidays.com/ecotourisme/?adherents_id=171 consulté le 5 février 2011.
4 http://www.inkaterra.com/en/reserva-amazonica/canopy-tree-house, consulté le 5 février 2011.

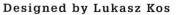
Designed by Lukasz Kos
Walker's Point, Lake Muskoka Ontario (Canada) — 2003

4tree house

This tree house is wrapped around four trees. The structure is surprising and open. It has three independent floor levels each with a different spatial configuration. Each level shares a view of Lake Muskoka and a deer reserve. A traditional local design, the Muskoka Balloon frame was used, although engineering was imported in the form of high-strength steel cables attached to each tree. Two Douglas fir beams are suspended from the cables and support the structure, which had a budget of $50 000, for a floor area of 40 square meters.

Das erstaunlich offen konzipierte Baumhaus wurde um vier Bäume gebaut. Seine drei eigenständigen Ebenen sind unterschiedlich konfiguriert. Jede von ihnen bietet Ausblick auf den Lake Muskoka und ein Rotwildreservat. Realisiert wurde die Konstruktion in Ständerbauweise als regionaltypisches Balloon-Frame-Fachwerk. Zusätzliche Stabilität gewinnt der Bau durch hochfeste Stahlkabel, die in den Bäumen verankert wurden. Zwei an Kabeln hängende Träger aus Douglasie stützen die Konstruktion, die mit einem Budget von 50 000 US-Dollar realisiert wurde und 40 m² Nutzfläche bietet.

Cette maison de structure étonnamment ouverte englobe les troncs de quatre arbres. Elle comprend trois niveaux indépendants, chacun d'une configuration spatiale particulière et bénéficiant d'une vue sur le lac Muskoka et une réserve de cerfs. Son créateur s'est inspiré d'un type constructif local, la charpente à claire-voie de Muskoka, mais a aussi fait appel à des solutions d'ingénierie plus contemporaine comme des câbles d'acier haute-résistance attachés à chaque arbre. Deux poutres en pin de Douglas suspendues aux câbles soutiennent cette maison dont la réalisation a coûté 50 000 $ pour une surface utile de 40 m².

Entirely supported by trees (right), the 4Tree House has a sophisticated regularity of form that is not common in such structures, surely because it is the work of a talented architect.

Das ausschließlich von Bäumen gestützte 4Tree House (rechts) ist formal von ungewöhnlicher Regelmäßigkeit – eine Seltenheit bei solchen Bauten–, zweifellos die Handschrift eines fähigen Architekten.

Reposant exclusivement sur des arbres, la maison 4Tree House (à droite) présente une régularité formelle exceptionnelle, une chose rare pour ce type de constructions et la marque indéniable d'un architecte de talent.

Lit from the interior at night, the 4Tree House glows like a giant lantern (left). Above, a view from the partially enclosed terrace.

Nachts leuchtet das Haus wie eine große Laterne (links). Oben ein Blick von der geschützten Loggia.

La nuit, la Maison aux 4 arbres fait penser à une lanterne géante (à gauche). Ci-dessus, vue de la terrasse en partie fermée.

Designed by Benoît Fray for Dans mon Arbre
2009

aerial village

This concept design boasts an interior floor area of 33 square meters with 17 square meters for the main room. There is a kitchenette, bath and toilet areas, and two bedrooms. Four to six people can be accommodated. The self-supporting structure with a larch frame is intended to integrate a tree, and would be hand-built in the Alps.

Der Konzeptentwurf verfügt über beeindruckende 33 m² Innenraum, von denen 17 m² auf den Hauptraum entfallen. Es gibt eine Kochnische, Bad und Toilette sowie zwei Schlafzimmer. Hier finden vier bis sechs Gäste Platz. Vorgesehen ist, die selbsttragende Konstruktion mit Lärchenholzrahmen in Bäume hineinzubau-en und in den Alpen von Hand zu errichten.

Ce projet encore à l'état de concept annonce une surface intérieure de 33 m² dont 17 pour la pièce principale. On trouve également une kitchenette, des sanitaires et deux chambres, l'ensemble prévu pour quatre à six occupants. Cette structure indépendante à ossature en mélèze qui pourrait s'intégrer dans un arbre devrait être construite artisanalement dans les Alpes.

In these computer-generated images, the Aerial Village is seen as a series of largely interconnected pods that are as much elevated platforms as they are veritable tree houses.

Simulationen zeigen das Village Aérien (dt. Schwebendes Dorf) als vielfach miteinander verbundene Module – darunter aufgeständerte Plattformen ebenso wie veritable Baumhäuser.

Dans ces images de synthèse, le Village aérien est présenté comme une séries de *pods* interconnectés qui sont autant des plates-formes surélevées que de véritables maisons dans les arbres.

Dans mon Arbre, Benoît Fray   **42**

03

Designed by Takashi Kobayashi
Okinawa (Japan) — 2005

beach rock tree house

The Beach Rock Tree House was built in 2005 as a feature of a resort for back-packing tourists on the island of Okinawa, which is a popular vacation spot for the Japanese. The designer calls it a "Plexiglass portal to the universe," and indeed, its structure allows visitors to see not only the trees around them, but also the sky. Because there is little private land with large trees in the urbanized areas of Japan, Kobayashi has sought out more rural locations for his work.

Das Beach Rock Tree House entstand 2005 als besonderes Highlight eines Ferienhotels für Rucksackreisende auf der Insel Okinawa, einem beliebten japanischen Reiseziel. Der Planer beschreibt seinen Entwurf als ein „Plexiglasfenster in den Weltraum" und tatsächlich haben Besucher von dort aus nicht nur einen Blick in die umstehenden Bäume, sondern in den Himmel. Da baumbewachsene Privatgrundstücke in japanischen Ballungsgebieten selten sind, sucht Kobayashi inzwischen bewusst ländlichere Standorte für seine Projekte.

Cette maison est une attraction dans une station pour randonneurs de l'île d'Okinawa, destination de vacances très populaire au Japon. Son concepteur parle « d'une porte de plexiglas ouverte sur l'univers » et cette structure permet en effet aux visiteurs non seulement d'observer la forêt mais aussi le ciel. Comme il n'y a pas beaucoup de terrains privés plantés de grands arbres dans les villes japonaises, Kobayashi a dû rechercher des sites plus ruraux pour ses créations.

Takashi Kobayashi is a former clothing buyer who became a professional tree house builder. He has become one of the most famous international figures in the area, precisely because of innovative designs like this one.

Takashi Kobayashi war Einkäufer in der Modebranche, bevor er eine Laufbahn als Baumhausdesigner einschlug. Dass er sich international als einer der bekanntesten Vertreter seiner Zunft profilieren konnte, liegt nicht zuletzt an so innovativen Entwürfen wie diesem.

Takashi Koyabashi est un ancien acheteur du secteur de la mode devenu constructeur de maisons dans les arbres. Il en est l'un des créateurs les plus célèbres dans le monde et précisément pour des projets novateurs du type de celui-ci.

Designed by Andreas Wenning (baumraum)
Osnabrück (Germany) — 2006

between alder and oak

Located in northwest Germany, this tree house was built, as its name indicates, between an alder and an oak. It has glazing on all sides and a large dormer window. An intermediate terrace is reached by a stairway, with the main cabin just a meter higher up. The interior is made with a large area for guests to lie in with glazing all around that allows for full views of the site and the sky, or the neighboring trees. Built-in furnishing is made of oak. Unlike some projects by Andreas Wenning, this realization has a tree crossing right through its deck.

Das in Norddeutschland gelegene Baumhaus wurde, wie der Name sagt, zwischen eine Erle und eine Eiche gebaut. Der rundum verglaste Bau hat außerdem eine große Lichtgaube. Eine Treppe führt zu einer Zwischenterrasse, die eigentliche Kabine liegt knapp einen Meter höher. Im Innern bietet eine große, von Fenstern gerahmte Liegefläche den Gästen einen Panoramablick auf die Umgebung, in den Himmel oder die umstehenden Bäume. Die Einbauten wurden aus Eiche gefertigt. Im Unterschied zu manch anderen Projekten von Andreas Wenning wächst hier ein Baum mitten durch die Terrasse.

Située dans le nord-ouest de l'Allemagne, cette maison perchée a été installée, comme son nom l'indique, entre un aulne et un chêne. Vitrée sur trois côtés, elle est aussi dotée d'une grande lucarne. On y accède par un escalier et une terrasse intermédiaire située à un mètre en dessous du niveau habitable. L'intérieur comprend un grand lit-podium entouré de baies vitrées qui offrent une vue panoramique sur le terrain, les arbres et le ciel. Le mobilier intégré est en chêne. Différente d'autres projets d'Andreas Wenning, la maison se distingue aussi par la mise en scène d'un arbre qui traverse la terrasse.

The rounded form of the tree house blends into its verdant background, offering sheltered spaces such as the terrace visible on the right, one meter below the cabin.

Mit seinen gerundeten Formen fügt sich das Baumhaus in die grüne Kulisse und bietet geschützte Plätze wie die Terrasse rechts im Bild, rund einen Meter unterhalb der Kabine.

La forme arrondie de la maison se fond dans son cadre verdoyant, tout en offrant des espaces abrités comme cette terrasse (à droite) située un mètre en contrebas.

Views in all directions give visitors the impression not only of being in the trees, but also of being protected as they observe nature from this privileged angle.

Der Panoramablick vermittelt den Besuchern nicht nur das Gefühl, zwischen den Bäumen zu schweben, sondern auch, aus dieser besonderen Warte die Natur geschützt beobachten zu können.

Des vues dans toutes les directions donnent aux visiteurs l'impression non seulement de se trouver au milieu des arbres, mais aussi de se sentir protégés pour observer la nature d'une position privilégiée.

05

Designed by Michael Ince
Bridgehampton, New York (USA)

bialsky
tree house

As the designer Pete Nelson points out, this is not a true tree house but "more of a stilt house." Like other works of the artist and sculptor Michael Ince, it is made of reclaimed wood, mainly pine. Ince uses a band saw to form the wood. This structure was built for Jay Bialsky and intended for use by his children. Bialsky is a local promoter and designer of luxury houses that are in contrast with the "Tolkienesque" design of this tree house.

Laut Pete Nelson, von dem dieser Entwurf stammt, handelt es sich hier nicht um ein Baumhaus, sondern „eher um ein Haus auf Stelzen". Realisiert wurde der Bau, wie andere Arbeiten des Künstlers und Bildhauers Michael Ince, vorwiegend aus Altholz, zumeist Kiefernholz. Für den Zuschnitt arbeitete Ince mit einer Bandsäge. Bauherr Jay Bialsky ließ das Haus für seine Kinder bauen: Das Tolkien'sche Baumhaus wirkt wie ein Kontrastprogramm zu den von Bialsky geplanten und angebotenen Luxusbauten.

Comme le fait remarquer le designer Pete Nelson, il ne s'agit pas d'une vraie maison dans les arbres mais « plutôt d'une maison sur pilotis. » Comme d'autres œuvres de l'artiste et sculpteur Michael Ince, celle-ci est en bois de récupération, principalement du pin. Ince découpe son bois à la scie à bande. La maison a été construite pour Jay Bialsky et surtout ses enfants. Bialsky est un promoteur et concepteur de maison de luxes qui n'ont rien à voir avec l'esprit « Tolkienesque » de ce projet.

Set up on stilts, the Bialsky Tree House has a fairy-tale appearance but it is not located near any trees. Children accede to it via the wooden ladder, and a simple swing hangs from the extended roof beam.

Das Bialsky-Baumhaus mit seinen Stelzen wirkt wie ein Märchenhaus, auch wenn es nicht zwischen Bäumen steht. Kinder erklettern das Haus über eine Leiter, an einem auskragenden Balken hängt eine einfache Schaukel.

Posée sur pilotis, cette maison de conte de fée, est éloignée de tout arbre. Les enfants y accèdent par l'échelle de bois. Une balance est suspendue à l'avancée de la poutre de faîtage.

Made with recuperated wood that is sawed by the designer Michael Ince, the house has a rough appearance but is both poetic and sophisticated in its concept.

Designer Michael Ince arbeitete mit Altholz, das er entsprechend zusägte. Das Haus wirkt rustikal, ein Entwurf, der ebenso poetisch wie anspruchsvoll gestaltet ist.

Fabriquée en planches de bois de récupération sciées par Michael Ince lui-même, cette maison d'apparence rustique est à la fois poétique et de conception sophistiquée.

06

Designed by David Greenberg, Tree Houses of Hawaii
Sanya, Hainan (China) — 2000

big beach in the sky tree house

Tree Houses of Hawaii built four tree houses near the new 2000-hectare Sanya Nanshan Buddhist and ecological theme park. Hainan is located to the south of the Chinese mainland and east of Hanoi. The Big Beach in the Sky Tree House was erected on two and a half levels in a large tamarind tree and is acceded to via a suspension bridge. It is set close to a beach on the South China Sea, and can be rented by the night for up to six people. The picturesque design of the tree house and its exotic location make this a particularly appealing realization. This tree house does have electricity but showers are a short walk away.

Das Büro Tree Houses of Hawaii baute vier Baumhäuser in der Nähe des neuen 2000 ha großen buddhistisch-ökologischen Sanya-Nanshan-Freizeitparks auf der Insel Hainan, südlich des chinesischen Festlands und westlich von Hanoi. Das Baumhaus Big Beach in the Sky mit seinen zweieinhalb Ebenen wurde in eine große Tamarinde gebaut und ist über eine Hängebrücke zugänglich. Das in Strandnähe am Südchinesischen Meer gelegene Haus kann nächteweise für bis zu sechs Personen gemietet werden. Besonders reizvoll sind der pittoreske Entwurf und der exotische Standort. Das Baumhaus hat keinen Stromanschluss, doch Duschen liegen nur einen kurzen Fußweg entfernt.

Tree Houses of Hawaii a construit quatre maisons dans les arbres près du nouveau parc à thème bouddhiste et écologique de 2000 ha de Sanya Nanshan à Hainan, dans l'extrême sud de la Chine. La maison dans l'arbre de la « Grande plage dans le ciel » de deux niveaux et demi est nichée dans un énorme tamarin auquel on accède par une passerelle suspendue. Construite non loin d'une plage de la mer de Chine méridionale, elle peut recevoir jusqu'à six personnes et se loue à la nuit. Sa conception pittoresque et sa situation exotique en font une création architecturale particulièrement attirante. Elle n'est pas équipée de l'électricité et les douches sont à proximité.

With its rustic appearance, the Big Beach in the Sky Tree House seems to be particularly well integrated with its verdant forest environment, and specifically with the tree in which it is built.

Das rustikale Baumhaus Big Beach in the Sky integriert sich gelungen in die bewaldete Umgebung, insbesondere in den Baum, in den es gebaut wurde.

D'aspect rustique, la maison de la Grande plage dans le ciel semble particulièrement bien intégrée dans son environnement boisé et dans son arbre.

The tree penetrates the structure entirely to the extent that the structure appears to be part of the wood of the tree itself.

Der Baum durchdringt die gesamte Konstruktion, sodass das Haus wie ein organischer Bestandteil des Astwerks wirkt.

L'arbre pénètre si profondément la structure qu'elle semble réellement en faire partie.

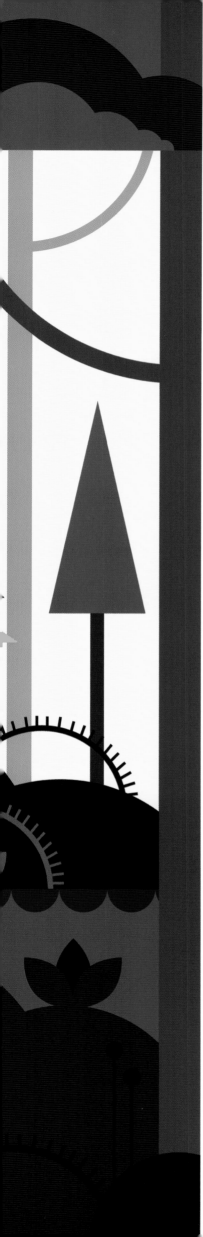

07

Designed by Inredningsgruppen
Harads (Sweden) — 2008

bird's nest
tree hotel

The exterior of this tree house was, indeed, designed to resemble a bird's nest. It has a retractable staircase which underlines its location well above the ground. There is an intentional contrast between interior and exterior with a 17-square-meter space that resembles a small, modern hotel room. Despite its "natural" appearance, the plan of the Bird's Nest forms a perfect circle. This is part of the Tree Hotel complex located in the far north of Sweden that includes structures by other architects.

Dieses Baumhaus soll von außen tatsächlich wie ein Vogelnest wirken. Eine Ausziehleiter unterstreicht seine Position hoch über dem Boden. Der Außenbau kontrastiert bewusst mit dem Innenraum: Der 17 m² große Raum ist ein kleines, modernes Hotelzimmer. Trotz seiner „natürlichen" Optik ist das Bird's Nest vom Grundriss her ein makelloser Kreis. Das Baumhaus gehört zum Tree-Hotel-Komplex in Nordschweden, der auch Bauten anderer Architekten umfasst.

L'extérieur de cette maison a été spécifiquement dessiné pour ressembler à un nid d'oiseau. Son escalier rétractable l'isole du sol. Le contraste entre l'extérieur et l'intérieur de 17 m² qui ressemble à une petite chambre d'hôtel moderne est évidemment volontaire. Malgré cet aspect « naturel », le plan de la maison est parfaitement circulaire. La maison fait partie du complexe Tree Hotel situé à l'extrême nord de la Suède, lequel comprend plusieurs maisons dans les arbres construites par d'autres architectes.

The scale and form of the Bird's Nest make it quite different from most tree houses—with its veritable function not immediately apparent. Access is through a retractable stairway.

Das Bird's Nest unterscheidet sich in Größe und Form von den meisten Baumhausbauten – seine Funktion erschließt sich nicht auf den ersten Blick. Zugang verschafft eine Ausziehleiter.

L'échelle et la forme du Nid d'oiseau le distinguent de celles de la plupart des maisons dans les arbres. Sa fonction n'est pas immédiatement apparente. L'accès se fait par un escalier rétractable.

The interior, with its relatively small porthole windows, is decidedly modern, with natural light also entering the space from above. Walls are clad in wood. The small space includes two sleeping areas, a bathroom, and living area as well.

Der Innenraum mit den vergleichsweise kleinen Bullaugenfenstern ist auffällig modern. Tageslicht fällt auch von oben ein. Die Wände wurden mit Holz vertäfelt. Der kleine Raum umfasst zwei Schlafbereiche, ein Bad und einen Wohnbereich.

L'intérieur aux hublots relativement petits est résolument moderne. Le volume éclairé par une verrière et habillé de bois contient deux zones de coucher, une salle d'eau et un petit séjour.

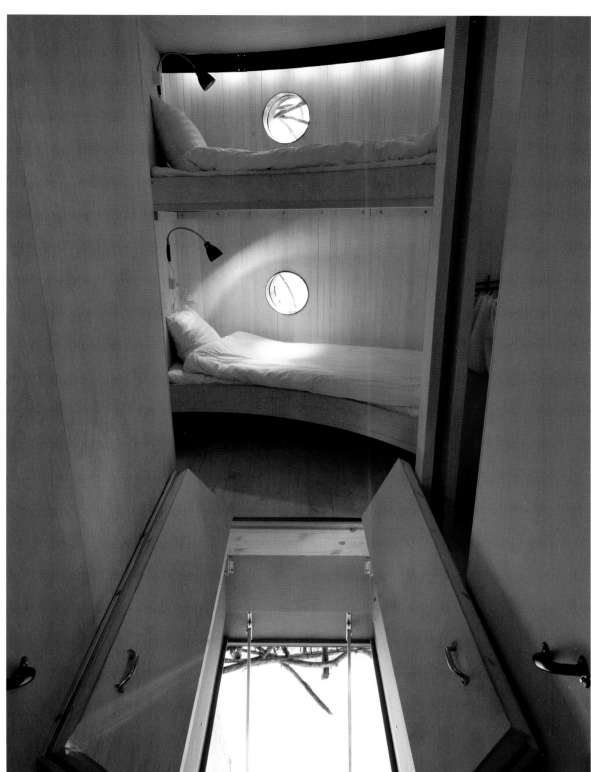

08

Designed by SandellSandberg
Harads (Sweden) — 2010

blue cone tree hotel

This 20-square-meter tree house is part of the Harads Tree Hotel in northern Sweden. It touches the ground at three points, which are the supports of the structure. It has four beds, a sleeping loft, a bathroom, and a living room. It has a lightweight wooden design with a split-birch shingle façade that is painted red. Access to the Blue Cone is via a wooden bridge. The windows and cupola of the structure are made of plastic. The Tree Hotel is open all year long.

Das 20 m² große Baumhaus ist Teil des Tree Hotels in Harads, Nordschweden. Mit ihren Stützen berührt die Konstruktion den Boden an drei Punkten. Untergebracht sind hier vier Betten, ein Hochbett, ein Bad sowie ein Wohnbereich. Der Leichtbau aus Holz mit einer Fassade aus Birkenholzschindeln ist rot gestrichen. Erschlossen wird der Blue Cone über eine Holzbrücke. Fenster und Oberlicht des Hauses sind mir Acryl verglast. Das Tree Hotel ist ganzjährig geöffnet.

Cette maison de 20 m² fait partie du Harads Tree Hotel situé dans le nord de la Suède et ouvert toute l'année. Elle touche le sol en trois points qui sont les soutiens de sa structure. Elle est équipée de quatre lits, d'une salle d'eau et d'un séjour. Légère et construite en bois, sa façade est habillée de shingles de bouleau peintes en rouge. On y accède par un pont de bois. Les fenêtres et la coupole sont en plastique.

The shingles used on the façades continue on the sloped roof of the Blue Cone tree house. The bridge leading to the tree house takes in a tree as though it were part of the structure.

Die Schindeln der Fassade ziehen sich bis zur Dachspitze des Blue-Cone-Baumhauses. Die Zugangsbrücke integriert einen Baum wie selbstverständlich in die Konstruktion.

Les shingles des façades sont dans la continuation de celles de la toiture. Le petit pont d'accès intègre un arbre comme s'il faisait partie du projet.

The living area of the Blue Cone brings to mind modern Swedish design more than a tree-house space. Wood, floors, and a large window give the impression of a more "normal" hotel than that of a hotel room lifted up on pilotis in the midst of the forest.

Der Wohnbereich im Blue Cone lässt eher an modernes schwedisches Design als an ein Baumhaus denken. Durch Holzverschalung, Dielen und ein großes Fenster entsteht eher der Eindruck eines „gewöhnlichen" Hotels als der eines auf Pilotis ruhenden Hotelzimmers mitten im Wald.

L'aménagement du séjour fait davantage penser à un intérieur suédois moderne qu'à une maison dans les arbres. Le bois, le plancher et une grande baie donnent plus l'impression d'être dans un hôtel « normal » que dans une chambre sur pilotis au milieu d'une forêt.

09

Designed by Mårten & Gustav Cyrén
Harads (Sweden) — 2008

cabin
tree hotel

Located on a steep slope, this structure was influenced by its site with a deck whose shape is related to the supporting trees. In a sense the actual tree house hangs from this deck. The architects write: "We played around with the angles and rounded off the corners lengthwise. It now looks like a capsule or cabin, an expression we feel comfortable with." The Cabin tree house is part of the complex of structures designed by other architects that form the Harads Tree House Hotel in northern Sweden.

Der an einem steilen Abhang gelegene Bau greift die Topografie des Geländes auf, seine Brücke zieht sich zwischen den tragenden Bäumen hindurch. Fast scheint es, als würde das Baumhaus an der Brücke hängen. Die Architekten schreiben: „Wir haben mit verschiedenen Perspektiven gespielt und die Ecken des Baus in Längsrichtung abgerundet. Jetzt wirkt das Ganze wie eine Raumkapsel oder eine Kabine, eine Optik, die uns gefällt." Das Cabin-Baumhaus gehört zum Komplex des Tree Hotel im nordschwedischen Harads, dessen Bauten von verschiedenen Architekten stammen.

Accroché au flanc d'une pente abrupte, ce projet a été influencé par son site : sa terrasse s'est adaptée aux arbres qui la soutiennent. D'une certaine façon, la maison est suspendue à cette terrasse. « Nous avons joué avec les angles et arrondi les coins sur toute la longueur », écrivent les architectes, « la maison a l'air d'une capsule ou d'une cabine, idée avec laquelle nous nous sentons à l'aise. » La Cabine, fait partie d'un ensemble de maisons dans les arbres conçues par divers architectes, qui constituent le Harads Tree House Hotel situé en Suède septentrionale.

With its long narrow approach bridge (below), the Cabin appears to hang in the trees without any visible means of support. It contrasts modern lines with its forest setting.

Mit seiner langen schmalen Zugangsbrücke hängt das Cabin-Baumhaus (unten) scheinbar stützenlos zwischen den Bäumen. Die moderne Linienführung ist ein bewusst gewählter Kontrast zur waldigen Umgebung.

Accessible par une longue et étroite passerelle (ci-dessous), la Cabane semble suspendue dans les arbres sans support visible. Ses lignes modernes contrastent avec le cadre de la forêt.

The room in the Cabin tree house measures 24 square meters in floor area. It accommodates two people and has a double bed, bathroom, and terrace.

Der Innenraum des Cabin-Baumhauses hat eine Grundfläche von 24 m². Er bietet Platz für zwei Personen und ist mit Doppelbett, Bad und Terrasse ausgestattet.

L'intérieur de la maison a une surface de 24 m². Équipée d'un lit double, d'une salle d'eau et complétée d'une terrasse, la Cabine est prévue pour deux personnes.

10

Designed by Inkaterra
near Puerto Maldonado, Tambopata (Peru)

canopy tree house

The Inkaterra Reserva Amazonica is in a 104-square-kilometer private ecological reserve in the Amazon rain forest, near the Tambopata National Park. A lodge and tree structures arrayed in the Inkaterra Canopy mark the site, weaving between trees that range in height between 30 and 60 meters. This system of bridges, platforms, and towers offers visitors a privileged view into the ecosystems of the rain forest. The Inkaterra Canopy is a non-profit NGO. Bolts running through tree trunks sustain each bridge. Solid vertical towers, special steel cables, beams, and the concept of the complex give it a life span of 30 years in the difficult tropical environment. The Canopy Tree House published here is built on a private platform 27 meters above the ground and is adjacent to the Canopy Walkway.

Das 104 km² große private Naturschutzgebiet Reserva Amazonica liegt in der Nähe des Tambopata Nationalparks. Die Ferienanlage Inkaterra umfasst ein Haupthaus und mehrere Baumhäuser, die in den 30 bis 60 m hohen Bäumen verteilt sind. Ein System aus Brücken, Terrassen und Türmen verbindet die Bauten und bietet den Gästen außergewöhnliche Einblicke in das Ökosystem des Regenwalds. Die Ferienanlage ist eine gemeinnützige NGO. Die Brücken sind an Bohrhaken in den Bäumen verankert. Dank der massiven Turmkonstruktionen, spezieller Stahlkabel und -träger und dem Planungskonzept hat der Komplex trotz schwieriger klimatischer Bedingungen eine geschätzte Lebensdauer von 30 Jahren. Das Canopy Tree House liegt auf einer privaten Plattform in 27 m Höhe, gleich neben dem Canopy Walkway.

La Reserva Amazonica est une réserve écologique privée de 104 km² dans la forêt pluviale amazonienne près du parc national de Tambopata. Le projet d'Inkaterra qui tisse un réseau aérien entre des arbres de 30 à 60 m de haut comprend une résidence et des constructions dispersées dans la canopée. Un système de passerelles, de plates-formes et de tours offre aux visiteurs une vue privilégiée sur l'écosystème de la forêt pluviale. Le projet de la Canopée d'Inkaterra est une ONG. Chaque passerelle est soutenue par des tiges de métal passées à travers les troncs. Des tours d'accès en bois, des câbles en acier spécial et le concept même devraient assurer à ce complexe une durée de vie d'une trentaine d'année dans son environnement tropical difficile. La maison présentée ici est construite sur une plate-forme privée à 27 m de hauteur, à côté de de la passerelle de la canopée.

Located 27 meters above the ground this tree house is unusually high. It is reached by a vertiginous stairway, seen from below on the right page.

Mit einer Höhe von 27 m liegt dieses Baumhaus ungewöhnlich hoch. Erschlossen wird es über eine schwindelerregende Treppe, auf der rechten Seite in Untersicht zu sehen.

Positionnée à 27 mètres au-dessus du sol, cette maison dans l'arbre n'est pas loin d'un record de hauteur. Un escalier vertigineux permet de l'atteindre (page de droite).

11

Designed by Lion Sands
Sabi Sand Game Reserve, Mpumalanga (South Africa)

chalkley tree house

This tree house was built on the site where Guy Aubrey Chalkley had set up camp to escape from predators in 1933. Chalkley created Lion Sands that year in the Sabi Sand Game Reserve, which is in the Kruger National Park. The designers call it a "bush bedroom," and it is, in fact, more a platform than a tree house in any traditional sense. It is built around a 500-year-old Leadwood tree. The structure houses a maximum of two people, who are able to view game that is free to wander through the reserve, which has no fences.

Standort des Baumhauses ist die Lagerstelle, an der Guy Aubrey Chalkley 1933 Zuflucht vor Raubtieren suchte – im gleichen Jahr gründete er Lion Sands im Wildschutzgebiet Sabi Sand im Kruger-Nationalpark. Die Planer des Chalkley Tree House sprechen von einem „Schlafzimmer im Busch" und tatsächlich handelt es sich eher um eine aufgeständerte Terrasse als um ein Baumhaus im üblichen Sinne. Erbaut um einen 500 Jahre alten Leadwood-Baum, bietet die Plattform Platz für zwei Gäste, die von hier das frei lebende Wild im Park beobachten können.

Cette maison dans l'arbre a été édifiée sur le site où l'ingénieur et agent de change Guy Aubrey Chalkley avait installé un camp pour se protéger des animaux prédateurs en 1933. Il avait créé la même année Lion Sands dans la réserve de chasse de Sabi Sand à l'intérieur du Parc national Kruger. Les auteurs du projet parlent d'une « chambre dans la brousse » car il s'agit davantage d'une plate-forme que d'une maison dans un arbre au sens habituel du terme. Appuyée contre un arbre de fer vieux de cinq siècles, elle ne peut accueillir que deux personnes qui peuvent observer les animaux se déplacer librement dans cette réserve sans barrières.

This tree house is exceptionally open, allowing guests to view wildlife directly and also to enjoy the remarkable outdoor scenery of the Sabi Sand Game Reserve.

Das Baumhaus ist ungewöhnlich offen. Die Gäste haben so freien Blick auf die Tierwelt und können die beeindruckende Landschaft des Wildschutzgebiets Sabi Sand genießen.

Cette maison particulièrement ouverte permet à ses hôtes d'observer directement la vie sauvage et le remarquable paysage de la réserve de chasse de Sabi Sand.

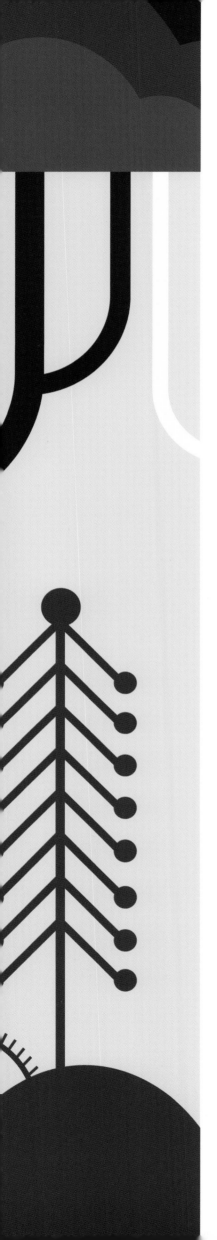

12

Designed by Schneider+Schumacher
Solingen (Germany) — 2009

clara's tree house

Schneider+Schumacher call this project "pocket-sized architecture for the garden to delight both adults and children." It is designed to fit into any garden and to be safely suspended from branches. It was built using weatherproof bonded wood panels made of 21-millimeter-thick Wisa spruce. Acrylic glazing brings ample daylight into the tree house. Clara's Tree House measures 3.4 x 3.4 x 2.3 meters and weighs 400 kilograms. It can carry a weight of up to 280 kilograms. Its cost was approximately €8500, but a special "spring edition" can be built for €5790.

Schneider+Schumacher beschreiben das Projekt als ein „Stückchen Baukultur für den Garten, an dem Groß und Klein Freude haben". Der Entwurf fügt sich in jeden Garten und lässt sich sicher in den Bäumen einhängen. Realisiert wurde die Konstruktion aus 21 mm starken Wisa-Spruce-Paneelen, wetterfesten verleimten Holzplatten. Dank seiner Acryl-Verglasung ist das Baumhaus ausgesprochen hell. Claras Baumhaus misst 3,4 x 3,4 x 2,3 m, wiegt 400 kg und kann mit einer Nutzlast von bis zu 280 kg belastet werden. Das Projekt kostete 8500 €, ist jedoch auch in einer speziellen „Frühjahrs-Edition" für 5790 € erhältlich.

Schneider+Schumacher qualifient ce projet « d'architecture de poche pour jardin, conçue pour le plaisir des adultes et des enfants ». Il a été étudié pour s'adapter à tous les types de jardins et d'arbres. La maison présentée a été réalisée en panneaux d'épicéa WISA de 21 mm d'épaisseur traités contre le vieillissement. Les baies sont fermées de plaques d'acrylique qui assurent un généreux éclairage naturel. De 3,4 x 3,4 x 2,3 m et de 400 kg, la maison peut supporter une charge de 280 kg. Son coût s'est élevé à 8500 € environ, mais une « édition de printemps » est proposée à 5790 €.

The very light appearance of the structure is due to the carefully planned use of thin wood, as well as the generous acrylic glazing that lets light in and gives views of the trees.

Seine besondere Leichtigkeit und Helligkeit verdankt der Bau den dünn gewählten Holzpaneelen sowie der großzügigen Acrylverglasung, die Licht einfallen lässt und Ausblick in die Bäume schafft.

L'aspect extrêmement léger de la maison est dû au recours étudié à des bois légers et aux panneaux d'acrylique qui assurent une grande transparence.

The form of the tree house is derived from the use of a 2 x 2-meter mattress that was rotated 45° in order to accommodate a bench.

Formaler Ausgangspunkt für das Baumhaus war eine 2 x 2 m große Matratze, die um 45° gegen den quadratischen Grundriss gedreht wurde, um rundum eine Sitzfläche zu schaffen.

La forme de la maison est directement liée au choix d'un matelas de 2 x 2 pivoté à 45° pour installer une banquette.

13

Designed by Andreas Wenning (baumraum)
New York (USA) — 2007

cliff
tree house

Located in Upstate New York near the Hudson River, this tree house is set near a cliff with a view of the river. The clients wanted the structure, built in a maple tree, to be large enough for parents and their two children. Rough larch planks painted silver were used on the exterior, while an oak terrace is attached to the tree with textile straps and stainless-steel cables. Approached from a ramp leading from the cliff, the terrace of the tree house is formed around the two largest branches of the maple. A catwalk leads from the 10.4-square-meter terrace to the 9.4-square-meter tree house. Untreated oak was used for interior surfaces. Generous glazing by the standards of most tree houses is augmented by an operable skylight. Like most of Andreas Wenning's tree houses, this structure combines modernity with obvious proximity to nature and generous views.

Das Baumhaus in Upstate New York liegt an einem Steilabhang mit Blick auf den Hudson River. Die Bauherren wünschten sich ein Haus in einem Ahorn, groß genug für Eltern und zwei Kinder. Der Außenbau aus unbehandelter Lärche wurde silbergrau gebeizt. Die über einen Steg erreichbare Terrasse ist mit Textilgurten und Edelstahlkabeln in den Baum gehängt und um die beiden Hauptstämme des Ahorns gebaut. Ein weiterer Steg verbindet die 10,4 m² große Terrasse mit dem 9,4 m² großen Baumhaus. Beim Innenausbau kam unbehandelte Eiche zum Einsatz. Die für Baumhäuser typische großzügige Verglasung wurde noch um eine Dachluke ergänzt, die sich öffnen lässt.

Située dans le nord de l'État de New York, à proximité de l'Hudson, cette maison dans un érable est positionnée au sommet d'une falaise dominant le fleuve. Les clients souhaitaient qu'elle puisse accueillir leur couple et leurs deux enfants. L'extérieur est habillé de planches de mélèze brut peintes de couleur argent. Une terrasse en chêne a été fixée dans l'arbre par des sangles textiles et des câbles d'acier inoxydable. Accessible par une rampe, la terrasse de 10,4 m² intègre deux des branches principales de l'érable. Une coursive conduit à la maison de 9,4 m² dont l'intérieur est en chêne non traité. Une baie vitrée de dimensions généreuses pour ce type de maison est complétée par une verrière zénithale. Comme la plupart des maisons dans les arbres de Andreas Wenning, celle-ci combine la modernité à la proximité réelle de la nature grâce à des ouvertures généreuses.

Supported by thin, inclined metal columns, the tree house is connected
to a wooden platform that is built around a neighboring tree. The structure is approached from a ramp, seen below.

Das Haus ruht auf schlanken, schrägen Metallpfählen und ist mit einer
Holzterrasse verbunden, die um einen nahe stehenden Baum gebaut
wurde. Erschlossen wird der Bau über einen Steg (unten im Bild).

Soutenue par de fines colonnes inclinées en métal, la maison est reliée
à une plate-forme de bois construite autour d'un arbre contigu. On y
accède par une rampe (ci-dessous).

The interior of the tree house is finished in untreated oak. The space, although small, like most tree houses, is agreeable and bright, with large glazed areas. The operable skylight is visible in the image on the left page (bottom).

Für den Innenausbau wurde mit unbehandelter Eiche gearbeitet. Wie bei den meisten Baumhäusern ist der Innenraum klein, dank großzügiger Verglasung jedoch einladend und hell. Das zu öffnende Oberlicht ist links unten im Bild.

L'intérieur de la maison est en chêne non traité. Bien que de faibles dimensions, comme dans la plupart des maisons de ce type, il est agréable et doté de grandes ouvertures. La verrière ouvrable apparaît également page de gauche (ci-dessous).

14

Designed by Andreas Wenning (baumraum)
Gross Ippener (Germany) — 2008

djuren tree house

Built in two oaks, it has a lower and upper terrace, the latter of which is perched 5.6 meters above the ground. Andreas Wenning states: "The rounded shape of this tree house is reminiscent of an egg cut open longitudinally. This association is heightened through the accenting of the gable surfaces with cream-painted Perspex, and the elliptically shaped windows." The terraces and underside of the tree house were made with indigenous oak, while sheet zinc was employed for the roof. Steel cables and textile straps are employed to suspend the structure in the tree. The terraces measure a generous 16.4 square meters, with the interior of the actual tree house covering 10.6 square meters.

Das in zwei Eichen gebaute Baumhaus verfügt über eine untere und eine obere Terrasse, die obere schwebt 5,6 m über dem Boden. Andreas Wenning schreibt: Die „gerundete Form" erinnert an ein „auf der Seite liegendes Ei", was „durch die Akzentuierung der Giebelflächen mit cremeweiß gestrichenem Acrylglas und die elliptisch geformte Fensterfläche weiter gesteigert" wird. Terrassen und Unterseite des Baumhauses wurden aus heimischem Eichenholz gebaut, das Dach ist mit Zinkblech eingedeckt. Die gesamte Konstruktion ist mit Stahlseilen und Textilgurten in den Bäumen eingehängt. Die Terrassen messen großzügige 16,4 m², auf den Innenraum des Baumhauses entfallen 10,6 m².

Construite dans deux chênes, cette maison possède une terrasse inférieure et une terrasse supérieure à 5,6 m au-dessus du sol. Comme l'explique Andreas Wenning : « La forme arrondie de la maison rappelle un œuf coupé longitudinalement. Cette association d'idée est renforcée par les pignons habillés de Perspex peint de couleur beige et les ouvertures elliptiques. » Les terrasses et le dessous de la maison sont en chêne local, le toit étant recouvert de zinc. La structure est accrochée aux arbres par des sangles textiles et des câbles d'acier. Les terrasses mesurent 16,4 m² de surface, l'intérieur de la maison 10,6 m².

Approached via a wooden ladder and an intermediate platform, the tree
house itself has a particularly modern form, with an unusual oval section. Supported by four thin steel columns, the tree house seems to float
in midair.

Das über eine Holzleiter und eine Zwischenplattform zugängliche
Baumhaus hat einen ungewöhnlichen ovalen Querschnitt. Der auf vier
schlanken Stahlstützen ruhende Bau scheint in der Luft zu schweben.

Accessible par une échelle de bois et une plate-forme intermédiaire, la
maison est de section ovale, de forme particulièrement moderne. Soutenue par quatre minces colonnes d'acier elle semble flotter dans l'air.

The oval section of the structure is translated by these large oval windows, and furniture that is built to accommodate the curving forms.

Die großen ovalen Fenster greifen den ovalen Querschnitt des Baus auf. Die Einbauten wurden in die geschwungene Form eingepasst.

La section ovale de la maison se retrouve dans les grandes ouvertures ovales et le mobilier intégré adapté aux courbes de la structure.

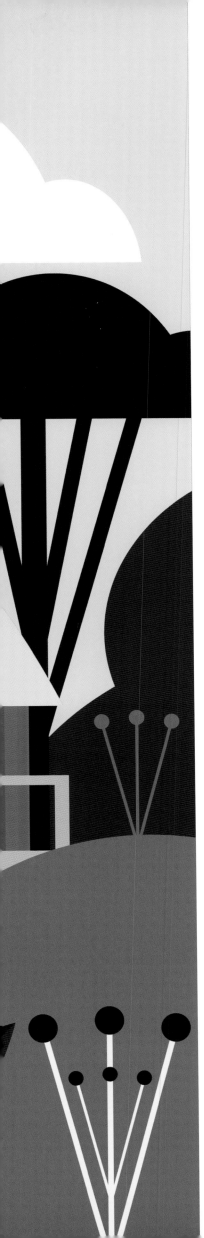

15

Designed by Pezulu Tree House Lodge
Limpopo (South Africa)

dream tree house

This large, thatched-roof structure is set up on wooden pilotis and is built between two Marula trees. It consists of a large main bedroom, a lounge, and a bathroom with jacuzzi bath. A separate walkway leads to a twin outdoor shower. The bed is built on wheels, allowing guests to sleep either inside or outside on the balcony under the stars. The large balcony of the Dream Tree House offers remarkable views of an African savannah and a waterhole.

Der große Reetdachbau ruht auf Holzpilotis und wurde zwischen zwei Marulabäumen errichtet. Er umfasst ein großes Schlafzimmer, ein Wohnzimmer sowie ein Bad mit Jacuzzi. Ein Steg führt zu einer Doppeldusche unter freiem Himmel. Das Bett auf Rollen überlässt den Gästen die Wahl, wo sie schlafen möchten: drinnen oder draußen auf der Terrasse unter den Sternen. Von Balkon und Terrasse des Dream Tree House haben die Gäste eine außergewöhnliche Aussicht auf die afrikanische Savanne und eine Wasserstelle.

Cette vaste construction à toit de chaume posée sur pilotis de bois est positionnée entre deux marulas. Elle contient un grand séjour, un salon et une salle de bains avec jacuzzi. Une passerelle conduit à deux douches jumelles extérieures. Le lit est monté sur roulettes permettant de dormir à l'intérieur ou sur le balcon à la belle étoile. L'important balcon offre des vues remarquables sur la savane africaine et un point d'eau.

This generous structure is characterized by its thatched roof and long, sloping approach ramp. Ideal for observing wildlife, the tree house has a twin outdoor shower, visible on the right (below).

Markante Merkmale des großzügigen Baus sind sein Reetdach und die lange Zugangsrampe. Das ideal zum Beobachten von Wildtieren geeignete Baumhaus hat eine Doppel-Außendusche (unten).

Cette généreuse construction, idéale pour observer la vie sauvage, se caractérise par son toit de chaume et sa longue rampe d'accès. Elle est équipée d'une double cabine de douche extérieure (ci-dessous).

Pezulu Tree House Lodge

The outdoor shower can be seen on the left page (top). The bed can be placed inside the tree house or on the generous terrace (above and left, bottom).

Links oben die Außendusche. Das Bett lässt sich im Innern des Baumhauses oder auf der großzügigen Terrasse platzieren (oben und links unten).

Les douches extérieures, page de gauche en haut. Le lit à roulettes peut être installé sur la grande terrasse (ci-dessus et à gauche, en bas).

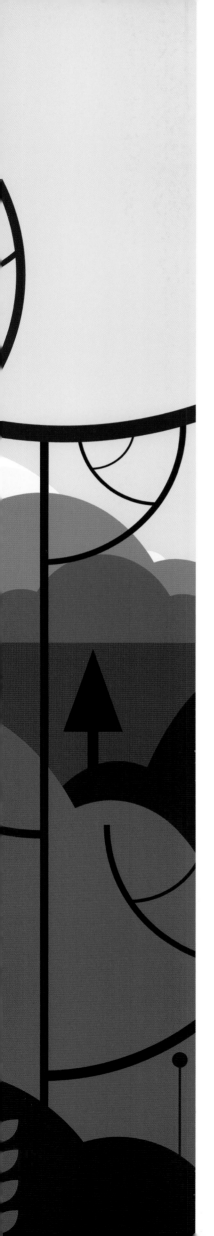

driftwood inn

This weekend house in a remote area of Puget Sound took almost 10 years to conceive according to Pete Nelson. The owner went so far as to work on 50 different designs before calling on Nelson. The completed structure, set between two century-old Douglas fir trees, one of which pokes through a deck, was baptized the Driftwood Inn by the children of the owner. A covered deck runs along the side and rear of the structure, with the rear part being entirely open to the sky. This large structure has a weight estimated at 61 000 kilograms (135 000 pounds).

Pete Nelson zufolge nahm die Planung dieses Wochenendhauses in der abgelegenen Gegend von Puget Sound fast zehn Jahre in Anspruch. Der Bauherr arbeitete an sage und schreibe fünfzig Entwürfen, bevor er Nelson beauftragte. Das Haus wurde zwischen zwei hundertjährigen Douglaskiefern gebaut (eine von ihnen wächst durch die Terrasse) und von den Kindern des Eigentümers auf den Namen Driftwood Inn getauft. Eine teilüberdachte Terrasse fasst Seiten und Rückseite des Baus ein, ihr rückwärtiger Teil liegt unter freiem Himmel. Die geräumige Konstruktion wiegt rund 61 000 kg.

D'après Pete Nelson, cette maison de week-end construite dans une zone isolée du Puget Sound a nécessité près de dix années de recherches. Son propriétaire avait travaillé sur 50 projets avant de faire appel à lui. La structure, édifiée entre deux pins de Douglas bicentenaires dont l'un traverse la terrasse, a été baptisée L'auberge du bois flotté par ses enfants. Une terrasse couverte court sur le côté et l'arrière de la maison, la partie arrière restant entièrement ouverte. Cette très importante construction pèse environ 61 tonnes.

Balanced between two trees, the house has an ample deck with curved edges—visible in the photo on the right on this page—with the side section protected by an extension of the roof.

Das zwischen zwei Bäumen schwebende Haus wird von einem großzügigen, geschwungenen Balkon umfangen – rechts im Bild –, dessen seitlicher Abschnitt von einem vorgezogenen Dach geschützt wird.

Fixée à deux arbres, la maison est partiellement entourée d'une terrasse aux angles arrondis, un des côtés étant protégé par une avancée du toit.

Driftwood logs and tree bark are used in the décor, but with its operating kitchen and bathroom, the tree house is certainly not without its comforts. Above, the upper-level bedroom; below, the seating area.

Im Interieur wurden Elemente aus Treibholz und Baumrinde integriert, doch mit einer voll funktionsfähigen Küche und einem Bad ist das Baumhaus sicher nicht ohne Komfort. Oben das Schlafzimmer im Obergeschoss; unten der Wohnbereich.

Des rondins de bois flotté et des écorces d'arbre participent à la décoration, mais cette maison équipée d'une cuisine et d'une salle de bains n'est certainement pas sans confort. Ci-dessus, la chambre de l'étage ; ci-dessous, le séjour.

17

Designed by Tom Chudleigh
Qualicum Bay, British Columbia (Canada) — 2007

free spirit spheres

Tom Chudleigh explains: "The Spherical Tree House concept borrows heavily from sailboat construction and rigging practice. It's a marriage of tree house and sailboat technology. Wooden spheres are built much like a cedar-strip canoe or kayak. Stairways hang from a tree much like a sailboat shroud hangs from the mast." The spheres are tethered to three different trees in order to spread the load, and can be hung anywhere between 1.5 and 30 meters off the ground. Electrical power is provided in the spheres which are outfitted with elements derived from yachting. They are 3.2 meters in diameter and are well insulated, allowing them to be used in temperatures as low as -20° C. Spheres named Eve, Eryn, and Melody are available for overnight rental on the site, which is located 30 kilometers north of Parksville on Vancouver Island.

Tom Chudleigh erklärt: „Konzeptuell ist das kugelförmige Baumhaus eng mit den Prinzipien von Bootsbau und Takelage verwandt. Die Holzkugeln werden wie Kanus oder Kajaks aus Zedernleisten gebaut. Die Treppen hängen am Baum wie Wanten am Mast." Um Lasten zu verteilen, werden die Kugeln mit Kabeln an drei Bäumen abgespannt. Sie lassen sich an beliebigen Standorten 1,5 bis 30 m über dem Boden aufhängen. Die mit Strom versorgten Kugeln sind mit Yachteinbauten ausgestattet. Die Häuser mit einem Durchmesser von 3,2 m sind stark gedämmt und bis zu -20 °C nutzbar. Drei Kugeln befinden sich auf Vancouver Island, 30 km nördlich von Parksville und können nächteweise gemietet werden.

Comme l'explique Tom Chudleigh : « Le concept de Maison dans l'arbre sphérique emprunte beaucoup à la construction navale et aux gréements. C'est un mariage de maison dans l'arbre et de technologie de la construction des voiliers. Les sphères en bois sont construites un peu comme un canoë ou un kayak en planches de cèdre. Les escaliers sont suspendus aux arbres comme les haubans au mât d'un voilier. » Les sphères sont accrochées à trois arbres pour répartir la charge et peuvent se suspendre n'importe où entre 1,5 m et 30 m au-dessus du sol. Elles sont équipées de l'électricité et d'éléments dérivés du yachting. De 3,2 m de diamètre, elles sont bien isolées ce qui permet de les utiliser même lorsque la température descend à moins 20° C. Nommées Eve, Eryn et Melody, elle sont louées à la nuitée sur ce site situé à 30 km au nord de Parksville sur l'île de Vancouver.

Approached via a spiral staircase with a rope design that confirms Tom Chudleigh's reference to boat structures, the tree house has an unexpected form that might recall an eyeball here.

Erreichbar über eine Wendeltreppe mit Seilelementen – eine Bezugnahme auf den Bootsbau, von dem Tom Chudleigh spricht –, hat dieses Haus ein besonders ungewöhnliches Design und erinnert an einen Augapfel.

Accessible par un escalier de cordes en spirale qui confirme la référence de Tom Chudleigh à la construction navale, la maison présente une forme surprenante rappelant celle d'un globe oculaire.

The interior of the tree house appears ample in these images, with obvious references to old ship design, such as the porthole windows and the door that certainly looks watertight.

Der Innenraum der Baumhäuser wirkt großzügig. Offenkundig sind hier wieder die Zitate klassischer Bootselemente etwa in Form von Bullaugen oder einer Tür, die zweifellos wasserdicht wirkt.

L'intérieur de la maison semple assez vaste sur ces images, et non sans références aux aménagements de bateaux anciens comme dans les hublots ou la porte étanche de coursive.

18

Designed by Andreas Wenning (baumraum)
Münster (Germany) — 2009

frog prince

This tree house, located in a small private garden in Münster, was designed for a couple. It includes a tatajuba wood terrace that is set on four stainless-steel poles. Steps and a catwalk lead visitors to the actual cabin. Covered with zinc sheets and a tatajuba underside, the interior has a surface area of 8.6 square meters. The terrace is 2.8 meters above ground level while the catwalk and cabin are set at a height of four meters. Eight asymmetrically arranged, leaning stainless-steel supports bear the load of the cabin. Aside from zinc and tatajuba, other construction materials are 20-millimeter ash boards used for the façades, and 60 millimeters of mineral insulation.

Das in einem kleinen privaten Garten in Münster gelegene Baumhaus Froschkönig wurde für ein Bauherrenpaar entworfen. Die Terrasse aus Tatajubaholz ruht auf vier Edelstahlstützen. Über eine kleine Treppe und einen Steg gelangen die Besucher zur eigentlichen Kabine. Der mit Zinkblech sowie an der Unterseite mit Tatajubaholz verkleidete Raum hat eine Nutzfläche von 8,6 m². Die Terrasse schwebt 2,8 m über dem Boden, während Steg und Kabine auf einer Höhe von 4 m liegen. Die acht asymmetrisch angeordneten schiefen Edelstahlstützen dienen als Tragwerk für die Kabine. Neben Zinkblech und Tatajubaholz kamen außerdem eine 20 mm starke Fassadenverschalung aus Esche sowie eine 60 mm starke mineralische Dämmung zum Einsatz.

Cette maison dans l'arbre installée dans un petit jardin privé de Münster, a été construite pour un couple. Elle comprend une terrasse en tatajuba reposant sur quatre piliers en acier inoxydable. La cabine de 8,6 m² habillée de zinc et de tatajuba, pour sa partie inférieure, est accessible par une échelle et une passerelle. La terrasse est suspendue à 2,8 m de hauteur et la cabine à 4 m. Huit piliers inclinés en acier inoxydable disposés asymétriquement supportent la charge de la cabine. En dehors du zinc et du tatajuba, on trouve d'autres matériaux comme des planches de frêne de 20 mm pour les façades et une couche d'isolation minérale de 60 mm d'épaisseur.

As is often the case, Andreas Wenning places his tree houses on very fine, tilted pilotis. The approach stairs and intermediate deck are of a straightforward design, while the structure itself is ovoid in section.

Andreas Wenning platziert seine Baumhäuser oft auf besonders schlanken, schrägen Pilotis. Während Treppe und Zwischendeck sehr schlicht gehalten sind, hat die Kabine einen ovoiden Querschnitt.

Comme souvent, Andreas Wenning installe ses maisons dans les arbres sur de très minces pilotis inclinés. L'escalier d'accès et la terrasse intermédiaire sont rectilignes, mais la structure même est de plan ovale.

The ovoid form of the tree house allows for the spectacular curved window seen above. Interior detailing is refined and monochromatic. A real modern hideaway! Although it measures less than nine square meters, the interior appears ample.

Durch die ovoide Form des Baumhauses war der Einbau eines spektakulär geschwungenen Fensters (oben) möglich. Die Details im Innenausbau sind Ton in Ton gehalten und ausgesprochen hochwertig: ein modernes Refugium. Trotz einer Fläche von weniger als 9 m² wirkt der Innenraum großzügig.

La forme ovoïde de la maison a permis la pose de fenêtres spectaculaires. Les finitions intérieures sont monochromes et raffinées. Une retraite moderne… Bien qu'il mesure moins de 9 m², l'intérieur semble spacieux.

19

Designed by Dustin Feider, O2
San Diego, California (USA) — 2007

geo donar tree house

Called the Geo Live Oak by the designer, this tree house is made with steel struts, cherry hardwood flooring, an HDPE (recycled plastic bottle) canopy, and an "entry/exit basket." The flooring material was leftover wood from the client's house renovation. The basket is raised and lowered with an electric winch. Dustin Feider explains: "Sitting just off of the master bedroom of the main house, the view from this oak tree perch reaches all the way across the valley, taking in the beautiful surrounding desert landscape and natural boulder outcroppings."

Das Baumhaus, ein Entwurf von Dustin Feider aus der Geo-Live-Oak-Serie, wurde mit Druckstreben, Hartholzdielen aus Kirschholz, einem Dach aus HDPE (recycelten Plastikflaschen) und einem „Zugangs-/Ausstiegskorb" realisiert. Die Dielen sind Materialreste von der Renovierung des Haupthauses. Der Korb wird über eine elektrische Winde hochgezogen und herabgelassen. Dustin Feider erklärt: „Dieser Hochsitz in einer Eiche liegt unmittelbar vor dem Hauptschlafzimmer des Wohnhauses, bietet Ausblick über das ganze Tal und die Gelegenheit, die Schönheit der Wüstenlandschaft und der natürlichen Felsformationen zu bewundern."

Cette maison appelée aussi Geo Live Oak par son concepteur, comprend une structure géodésique en acier, un sol en cerisier, un habillage en HDPE (recyclage de bouteilles de plastique) et un « panier d'entrée/sortie ». Le bois du sol a été récupéré lors de la rénovation de la maison du propriétaire. Le panier monte et descend au moyen d'un treuil électrique. Comme Dustin Feider l'explique : « [La maison dans l'arbre est] positionnée tout près de la chambre principale de la maison, on découvre depuis les branches du chêne une vue qui couvre toute la vallée jusqu'au magnifique paysage du désert et de ses affleurements rocheux. »

The basic structure of this tree house is inspired by the geodesic domes of Buckminster Fuller. Approached from below, its triangulated form provides for generous daylight and openings toward the natural environment.

Die Grundkonstruktion des Baumhauses ist inspiriert von Buckminster Fullers geodätischen Kuppeln. Der Bau wird von unten erschlossen. Dreieckige Fassadenelemente und Öffnungen lassen reichlich Tageslicht einfallen und öffnen den Bau zur Natur.

La structure est inspirée des dômes géodésiques de Buckminster Fuller. Ses formes triangulaires permettent un généreux éclairage naturel et d'aménager des ouvertures sur l'environnement.

The tree house glows from within at night (above) and is filled with light during the day. The interior space is relatively simple, allowing for flexible use of the tree house depending on its occupants.

Nachts leuchtet das Baumhaus von innen (oben), tagsüber wird es durch Tageslicht erhellt. Der Innenraum ist schlicht gehalten und ermöglicht den Besuchern eine flexible Nutzung.

La nuit, la maison semble scintiller (ci-dessus). De jour, elle est baignée de lumière. L'espace intérieur est relativement simple et permet un usage souple en fonction du nombre de ses occupants.

20

Designed by Anya Meran for Dans mon Arbre
Vedène (France) — 2007

green pavilion tree house

Built 4.6 meters off the ground on a site near Avignon, the Green Pavilion is a guest house with a seven-square-meter terrace and 20 square meters of interior space. Built between two oak trees, the structure is supported by wooden pilotis. The exterior cladding is in pine, and the project cost was €40 000. The prefabricated structure includes a kitchenette and bathroom, and was hoisted into place with the use of a zip line.

Der Pavillon Vert (Grüne Pavillon) in der Nähe von Avignon wurde 4,6 m über dem Boden errichtet. Das Baumhaus mit einer 7 m² großen Terrasse und einem 20 m² großen Innenraum wird als Gästehaus genutzt. Der zwischen zwei Eichen errichtete Bau ruht auf Holzpilotis. Der Außenbau wurde mit Kiefernholz verkleidet, die Gesamtkosten des Projekts beliefen sich auf 40 000 €. Die vorgefertigte Konstruktion ist mit einer Küchenzeile und einem Bad ausgestattet und wurde mit einer Seilrutsche in Position gebracht.

Construit à 4,6 m du sol sur un terrain non loin d'Avignon, le Pavillon vert est une maison d'hôtes de 20 m² à terrasse de 7 m². Construite entre deux chênes, la structure habillée extérieurement de pin repose sur des pilotis de bois. Le coût de réalisation s'est élevé à 40 000 €. Cette construction préfabriquée qui comprend aussi une kitchenette et une salle d'eau, a été mise en place à l'aide d'une tyrolienne.

With its picturesque double-slanted roof and rather formal approach stairway, this tree house has all the makings of a real residence in the forest. A terrace big enough for two is seen below.

Mit seinem Giebeldach und dem eher förmlichen Treppenaufgang wirkt das Haus wie eine veritables Wohnhaus im Wald. Unten im Bild eine kleine Terrasse mit genug Platz für zwei Personen.

Par sa toiture pittoresque à pignon et son escalier assez formel, cette maison a toutes les apparences d'une véritable résidence en forêt. Ci-dessous, son assez grande terrasse.

Dans mon Arbre, Anya Meran   **156**

The interior is rustic in style but comfortable and includes a bathroom. Wood is used throughout, giving a continuity with the structure of the tree house and unifying its interior.

Das rustikale Interieur ist komfortabel und verfügt über ein Bad. Überall kommt Holz zum Einsatz, was nicht nur an die Holzkonstruktion des Hauses anknüpft, sondern auch für Harmonie im Interieur sorgt.

L'intérieur, qui comprend une salle d'eau, est de style rustique mais confortable. Il est entièrement en bois, en continuité avec la structure de la maison.

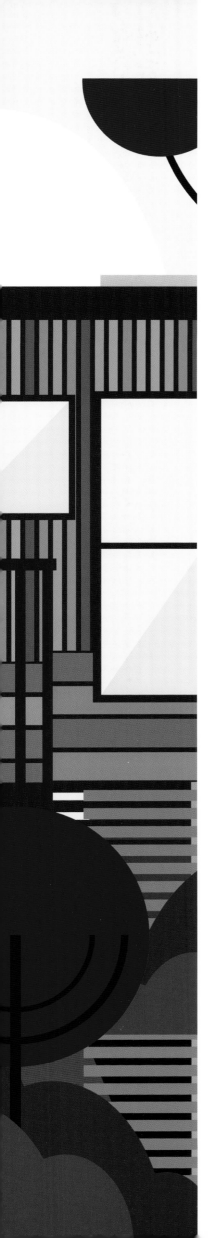

21

Designed by Hapuku Lodge
Kaikoura (New Zealand)

hapuku lodge tree houses

Hapuku Lodge is located 10 kilometers north of Kaikoura, on the east coast of South Island, overlooking the Seaward Mountain Range and Mangamaunu Bay. There are five "tree house" structures associated with Hapuku Lodge, though these are closer to "real" buildings than most of the tree houses published in this book. In part because of seismic risks, the tree houses are, in fact, perched on steel girders. The tree houses are, however, located 10 meters above ground level amongst manuka trees. The structures have views through generous windows of the spectacular natural setting. They are clad in native woods and copper shingles.

Die Hapuku Lodge liegt 10 km nördlich von Kaikoura, an der Ostküste der neuseeländischen Südinsel mit Blick auf die Seaward Kaikoura Range und die Mangamaunu-Bucht. Zur Hapuku Lodge gehören fünf „Baumhäuser", die „regulären" Wohnbauten ähnlicher sind als die meisten Baumhäuser in diesem Band. Die Baumhäuser ruhen, unter anderem aufgrund von Erdbebengefahr, auf Stahlträgern, schweben jedoch 10 m über dem Boden zwischen den Manuka-Bäumen. Dank großzügiger Verglasung bieten die Häuser Ausblick auf die spektakuläre landschaftliche Umgebung. Verschalt wurden die Bauten mit einheimischen Holzarten und Kupferschindeln.

Hapuku Lodge, à 10 km au nord de Kaikoura sur la côte orientale de l'île du Sud, donne sur la chaîne montagneuse de Seaward et la baie de Mangamaunu. Cinq « maisons dans les arbres » ont été aménagées à proximité de l'hôtel, bien qu'elles soient plus proches de constructions « classiques » que la plupart des projets publiés ici. Du fait des risques sismiques, elles sont perchées sur des poutrelles d'acier, mais ne s'en élèvent pas moins à 10 m au-dessus du sol parmi les manukas. Grâce à leurs généreuses ouvertures, elles offrent une vue spectaculaire sur leur environnement. Elles sont habillées de shingles en bois locaux et de cuivre.

Although the Hapuku Lodge Tree Houses are technically more like "real" architecture, they are nonetheless very much perched in the trees, offering a bird's eye view of the natural surroundings.

Zwar wirken die Baumhäuser der Hapuku Lodge eher wie „reguläre" Architektur, doch schweben sie hoch zwischen den Baumwipfeln und bieten Ausblick aus der Vogelperspektive auf die landschaftliche Umgebung.

Bien que ces maisons se rapprochent beaucoup de l'architecture « réelle », elles n'en sont pas moins perchées dans les arbres et offrent une vue plongeante sur leur cadre naturel.

The architectural design here is more sophisticated than what might be expected of a real tree house—indeed, the five Hapuku Lodge Tree Houses are like individual residences in the trees. Wood predominates in the exterior and interior finishes and generous views are available all around.

Die Architektur ist deutlich anspruchsvoller als man von einem Baumhaus erwarten würde – tatsächlich sind die fünf Baumhäuser der Hapuku Lodge eigenständige Wohnbauten zwischen den Bäumen. Holz dominiert Außen- wie Innenbau, die Aussicht ist in alle Richtungen unverstellt.

La conception architecturale des cinq maisons de Hapuku Lodge est plus sophistiquée que dans une maison dans les arbres habituelle, se rapprochant de celle d'une véritable résidence perchée. Le bois prédomine aussi bien à l'extérieur qu'à l'intérieur. Les ouvertures multiplient les vues.

22

Designed by Gilles and Dans mon Arbre
Sainte Beaume (France) — 2008

hermitage tree house

Intended for rental, this isolated structure can either be located at ground level or suspended in the trees. Its floor area is 6.8 square meters. Stained larch or other woods can be employed. The model presented here costs €10 500, and the designers aim to build future versions with industrial methods that would permit a substantial reduction in cost. Hatches and doors can be opened entirely, and most of the interior space is taken up by a comfortable bed.

Die isoliert gelegene Hütte mit einer Nutzfläche von 6,8 m² kann ebenerdig oder als Baumhaus realisiert werden und ist zur Vermietung vorgesehen. Für die Konstruktion eignen sich gebeizte Lärche und andere Holzarten. Die Kosten für das Musterhaus beliefen sich auf 10 500 €, doch die Planer arbeiten an verschiedenen Fertigbauversionen, die erhebliche Einsparungen ermöglichen sollen. Klappen und Fensterläden lassen sich vollständig öffnen; der Großteil des Innenraums wird von einem bequemen Bett eingenommen.

Destinée à la location, cette construction de 6,8 m² – présentée ici isolée en forêt – peut soit rester au sol soit être suspendue dans un arbre. Elle est réalisable en mélèze teinté ou dans d'autres bois. Le modèle présenté coûte 10 500 € et ses initiateurs projettent de le fabriquer selon des processus industriels qui permettraient d'en réduire substantiellement son coût. Les volets et les portes peuvent s'ouvrir entièrement et l'essentiel de l'espace est occupé par un lit confortable.

The structure allows a conversion from a totally closed form to one that is open literally on all sides. Not substantially lifted off the ground, the Hermitage is nonetheless very much in the trees.

Die Konstruktion erlaubt verschiedene Konfigurationen von vollständig geschlossen bis hin zur allseitigen Öffnung. Obwohl das Hermitage-Baumhaus nur geringfügig über dem Boden liegt, schwebt es doch zwischen den Bäumen.

La construction peut passer de l'état fermé à un état totalement ouvert. Légèrement surélevée par rapport au sol, elle ne s'en trouve pas moins dans les arbres.

Dans mon Arbre, Gilles   **170**

23

Designed by Dustin Feider, O2
Beverly Hills, California (USA) — 2009

honey sphere tree house

The Honey Sphere was exhibited on the grounds of the Los Angeles County Museum of Art before being installed on the property of Robby Krieger, the guitarist of the Doors. The musician wanted a place to relax and observe nature. The structure has 210 openings and 420 facets. The floor of the tree house was made with wood recuperated from the construction. The Honey Sphere is suspended from the upper branches of a live oak with a steel cable system that insures the protection of the tree. Installed in September 2009, it is 6.1 meters in diameter and has an area of 18.6 square meters. It was made with second-growth redwood and steel hubs.

Das Honey Sphere Baumhaus wurde zunächst am Los Angeles County Museum of Art ausgestellt und schließlich auf dem Grundstück von Robby Krieger, dem Gitarristen der Doors, permanent installiert. Der Musiker hatte sich einen Ort zum Entspannen in der Natur gewünscht. Die Konstruktion mit 420 Facetten hat 210 Öffnungen. Der Boden des Baumhauses wurde aus Altholz gefertigt, das bei den Bauarbeiten abfiel. Das Haus ist mit einem baumschützenden Stahlkabelsystem in den oberen Ästen einer Eiche aufgehängt. Die Kugel, im September 2009 gebaut, hat einen Durchmesser von 6,1 m, eine Nutzfläche von 18,6 m² und wurde aus aufgeforstetem Küstenmammutbaum und Stahlknotenpunkten realisiert.

Cette « ruche sphérique » a été exposée devant le Musée d'art du comté de Los Angeles avant d'être installée en septembre 2009 chez son propriétaire, Robby Krieger, le guitariste des Doors. Le musicien souhaitait un lieu pour se détendre et observer la nature. La structure de 6,1 m de diamètre et de surface intérieure utile de 18,6 m² présente 420 facettes et 210 ouvertures. Elle a été réalisée en séquoia de seconde venue et tubes d'acier. Le sol intérieur est en bois de construction récupéré. Elle est suspendue aux branches supérieures d'un chêne par un système de câbles qui limite les tensions sur l'arbre.

The structure of the Honey Sphere is entirely open to the elements.
Although it is suspended, it wraps around the tree and rests partially
on the ground in these images.

Das Honey Sphere Baumhaus ist vollkommen offen den Elementen ausgesetzt. Obwohl die Konstruktion aufgehängt ist, umfängt sie den Baum
und setzt teilweise auf dem Boden auf, wie diese Bilder zeigen.

La structure de l'Honey Sphere est entièrement ouverte aux éléments.
Bien que suspendue, elle entoure l'arbre, mais repose en partie sur le sol.

The pine floor of the Sphere is printed in a mandala pattern. Holes allow branches of the tree to penetrate the floor (above). Right, an exterior view and a detail of a structural node. Each diamond-shaped element was assembled and slipped over the tree branches.

Den Kiefernholzboden der Kugel schmückt ein Mandalamuster. Äste durchdringen den Boden (oben). Rechts eine Außenansicht sowie eine Detailaufnahme der Knotenpunkte. Jedes der diamantförmigen Segmente wurde einzeln zusammengefügt und über die Äste geführt.

Le sol en pin est décoré de motifs de mandalas. Les branches du chêne traversent le sol (ci-dessus). À droite, vue de l'intérieur et d'un nœud d'assemblage. Chaque élément a été assemblé et glissé à travers les branches.

24

Designed by Horace Burgess
Crossville, Tennessee (USA)

horace's cathedral

Also called the Minister's House, this may be the largest tree house in the world, measuring 30 meters in height; it has no less than 10 stories and is built around six trees. Its builder, Horace Burgess, explains that he began work on this edifice in 1993 after having a vision. He has stated: "I was playing one day, and the Lord said, 'If you build me a tree house, I'll see you never run out of material.'" Fourteen years later, the substance of the vision of Horace Burgess appears to have been fulfilled. "It's God's tree house," he says, "He keeps watch over it."

Der Bau, auch The Minister's House (Haus des Predigers) genannt, ist möglicherweise das größte Baumhaus der Welt. Das Haus ist 30 m hoch, hat nicht weniger als zehn Etagen und wurde um sechs Bäume gebaut. Bauherr Horace Burgess beschreibt, wie er die Arbeit am Baumhaus 1993 aufnahm, nachdem er eine Vision hatte: „Eines Tages, ich betete gerade, sagte mir der Herr: ‚Wenn du mir ein Baumhaus baust, will ich dafür sorgen, dass es dir nie an Material fehlt.'" Vierzehn Jahre später scheint es, als habe sich die Vision von Horace Burgess erfüllt. „Es ist Gottes Baumhaus", so der Prediger, „es steht unter seinem Schutz."

Également appelée the Minister's House (la maison du pasteur), c'est sans doute la plus grande maison dans les arbres au monde. Elle mesure 30 m de haut, ne compte pas moins de dix niveaux et est construite autour de six arbres. Son constructeur, Horace Burgess explique qu'il a commencé à travailler sur ce projet en 1993 après avoir eu une vision : « Je jouais un jour et le Seigneur m'a dit : » Si tu me construis une maison dans les arbres, je ferai en sorte que tu ne manque jamais de matériaux «. » Quatorze années plus tard, la vision s'est matérialisée. « C'est la maison dans les arbres de Dieu. Il la surveille », conclut Horace Burgess.

From a distance (right) the tree house looks very much like a church, but its mass and complexity are the very personal invention of its designer and builder.

Aus der Ferne (rechts) wirkt das Haus fast wie eine Kirche, doch Monumentalität und Komplexität des Baus zeugen von der höchst eigenen Handschrift seines Planers und Baumeisters.

À distance (à droite), la maison se présente comme une église, mais sa masse et sa complexité relèvent de l'inventivité très personnelle de son concepteur et constructeur.

Horace Burgess estimates that the tree house has a total floor area between 740 and 930 square meters. The structure cost $12 000 to build. Right, chimes in the tower made from oxygen acetylene bottles.

Horace Burgess schätzt die Nutzfläche des Baumhauses auf zwischen 740 und 930 m². Die Baukosten beliefen sich auf 12 000 Dollar. Aus alten Sauerstoffflaschen entstand das Windspiel im Turm (rechts).

Horace Burgess estime la surface de sa maison entre 740 et 930 m². Le projet a coûté 12 000 $. À droite, dans la tour, un carillon fait de bouteilles d'oxygène.

25

Designed by Terunobu Fujimori
Beipu (Taiwan) — 2010

irisentei tea nest

Built on bamboo props 7.2 meters above ground level, the Tea Nest has a floor area of 3.5 square meters. It is a monocoque structure built of plywood. Intended for drinking Chinese tea, this tree house is not submitted to the rather strict rules that generally govern traditional Japanese teahouses. The structure is built in a "giant bamboo" tree which can reach a height of 20 meters and a diameter of 20 centimeters. Terunobu Fujimori explains how this type of tree influenced the design: "One thing to be regretted is its weakness compared with other kinds of bamboos traditionally used in architecture. Considering the above, five bamboo props were used and the teahouse was put on them at a height of 7.2 meters. In order to decrease weight, its structure is of panelized plywood. It was assembled on the ground and lifted up by crane."

Das 7,2 m über dem Boden schwebende Tea Nest hat eine Nutzfläche von 3,5 m². Das Baumhaus wurde in Schalenbauweise aus Sperrholz realisiert. Obwohl man hier chinesischen Tee trinken kann, entspricht der Bau nicht den strengen Regeln japanischer Teehäuser. Der Bau ruht auf den Stämmen eines „Riesenbambus" – Pflanzen, die bis zu 20 m hoch werden und einen Durchmesser von bis zu 20 cm erreichen können. Fujimori schildert, wie die Baumart seinen Entwurf beeinflusste: „Einziger Nachteil ist die geringe Belastbarkeit im Vergleich zu anderen Bambusarten, die im Hausbau zum Einsatz kommen. Entsprechend wurden fünf Bambusstämme verwendet, um das Haus in 7,2 m Höhe aufzuständern. Er wurde am Boden montiert und mithilfe eines Krans in Position gehoben."

Monté sur des piliers de bambou à 7,2 m au-dessus du sol, ce Nid à thé offre une surface utile de 3,5 m². Prévue pour la dégustation du thé de Chine, il ne répond pas aux règles strictes qui gouvernent généralement la cérémonie du thé au Japon. C'est une structure monocoque en contreplaqué. Les piliers sont en une variété de bambou géant qui peut atteindre 20 m de haut pour un diamètre de 20 cm. Terunobu Fujimori explique comment ce type d'arbre a influencé son projet : « On peut regretter sa faiblesse de résistance par comparaison avec d'autres types de bambous utilisés en architecture et donc, dans ce projet, cinq piliers ont été nécessaires … Pour réduire le poids, la structure est en panneaux de contreplaqué. Elle a été assemblée au sol et mise en place par une grue. »

Like much of the architecture of Terunobu Fujimori, this tree house has more than a little humor in its design. Improbably high and small, it seems to come out of a child's fantasy.

Wie viele Bauten Fujimoris ist auch bei diesem Baumhaus mehr als deutlich ein Augenzwinkern zu spüren. Fast absurd hoch und klein wirkt das Häuschen wie eine Kinderfantasie.

Comme beaucoup de réalisations de Terunobu Fujimori, cette maison ne manque pas d'humour. Incroyablement haut perchée et petite, elle semble sortir de l'imagination d'un enfant.

Fujimori's work is a subtle mixture of references to Japanese culture and an offbeat sense of modernity. Though not technically built in a tree, the house has all the other qualities of a tree house. Above, the interior.

Fujimoris Arbeiten sind eine subtile Mischung aus japanischer Kultur und einem zeitgenössischen, wenn auch exzentrischen Stil. Zwar wurde das Haus nicht in einen Baum gebaut, dennoch hat es alle typischen Merkmale eines Baumhauses. Oben ein Blick ins Interieur.

L'œuvre de Fujimori est un subtil mélange de références à la culture japonaise et de modernité originale. Bien qu'elle ne soit pas technique-ment une maison dans les arbres, elle en possède toutes les qualités. Ci-dessus, l'intérieur.

26

Designed by Andreas Wenning (baumraum)

jungle house

This is a virtual project that stretches the definition of the tree house to reach what must be considered a thoroughly modern form of expression. It is organically shaped and entirely white, with an interior that can only be described as luxurious, with such features as a dining area, or a whirlpool bath. A number of thin metal supports are used to prop the structure high in the trees, with the tree actually bearing only the weight of the terrace. Andreas Wenning states: "The space, with its curved walls and ceilings, is oriented to the sea, or perhaps to a river on the edge of the tropical rain forest. It could also be on a mountain slope, opening itself up to a valley."

Das visionäre Projekt mit seiner ausgesprochen modernen Formensprache geht deutlich über typische Vorstellungen von einem Baumhaus hinaus. Der organische, ganz in Weiß gehaltene Bau hat ein luxuriöses Interieur mit Essbereich und Whirlpool. Gestützt wird die zwischen den Baumwipfeln schwebende Konstruktion von schlanken Metallstützen, nur die Terrasse wird von einem Baum getragen. Andreas Wenning erklärt: „Der Raum mit seinen geschwungenen Wand- und Deckenflächen orientiert sich zum Meer oder vielleicht zu einem Fluss am Rand eines tropischen Regenwaldes. Er könnte auch gut an einem Berghang stehen und sich zu einem Tal hin öffnen."

Ce projet virtuel étend la définition de la maison dans les arbres à ce que l'on pourrait considérer comme une expression architecturale résolument contemporaine. De forme organique, de couleur blanche, son intérieur équipé, par exemple d'un coin-repas ou d'un bain à remous, peut être qualifié de luxueux. Quelques fins piliers de métal soulève la structure entre les arbres, ceux-ci ne supportant que le poids de la terrasse Andreas Wenning précise : « L'espace intérieur dont les murs et les plafonds sont traités en courbes, est orienté vers la mer ou peut-être une rivière en limite d'une forêt tropicale. La maison pourrait également être édifiée en montagne, donnant sur une vallée. »

As in many of the built works of baumraum, this design is set up on stilts and has a rather futuristic appearance. Here, in computer-generated renderings, the tree house is placed in a tropical beach environment.

Wie viele realisierte Bauten von baumraum wirkt auch dieser Entwurf auf Stelzen recht futuristisch. Die computergenerierten Renderings versetzen das Baumhaus an einen tropischen Strand.

Comme dans beaucoup de réalisations de baumraum, ce projet sur pilotis présente un aspect assez futuriste. Dans cette image d'ordinateur, la maison a été imaginée dans un environnement de plage tropicale.

Again, bringing to mind realizations of Andreas Wenning, the interior of the Jungle tree house is curvilinear and modern in its concept. Large openings integrate the structure into its setting.

Auch das Interieur des Dschungelhauses mit den geschwungenen Linien und seinem modernen Konzept erinnert an realisierte Projekte Wennings. Große Öffnungen binden den Bau in sein Umfeld ein.

Rappelant plusieurs réalisations d'Andreas Wenning, l'intérieur tout en courbes est de conception très actuelle. De grandes ouvertures intègrent le cadre naturel.

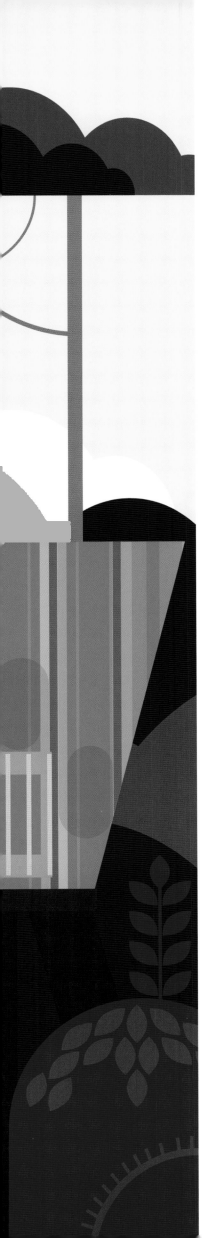

27

Designed by Renaud Morel for Dans mon Arbre
Eindhoven (The Netherlands) — 2010

kapellerput tree house

This structure is intended as a space for receptions, seminars, and ceremonies. It has a meeting space and two smaller work rooms, a kitchenette-bar, and a terrace. It is built at heights between 3.5 and 6 meters above the ground, and contains a total of 160 square meters of space, of which 65 square meters is the terrace. Wooden pilotis support the structure that is made of larch, Douglas fir, and pine. The walls lean outward at an angle of 7°. The total cost of the project was €350 000, of which the designers' share was €200 000.

Das Baumhaus wird als Raum für Empfänge, Seminare und Feierlichkeiten genutzt. Hier gibt es einen Konferenzbereich und zwei kleinere Arbeitsräume, einen Küchenbereich mit Bar sowie eine Terrasse. Der Bau liegt zwischen 3,5 und 6 m hoch über dem Boden und bietet insgesamt 160 m² Nutzfläche, 65 m² entfallen auf die Terrasse. Holzpilotis stützen den Bau aus Lärche, Douglasie und Kiefernholz. Die Wände sind mit 7° leicht nach außen geneigt. Die Gesamtkosten des Projekts beliefen sich auf 350 000 €, hiervon entfielen 200 000 € auf die Planung.

Ce projet a été conçu pour accueillir des réceptions, des séminaires et des cérémonies. Il possède une salle de réunion et deux petites salles de travail, un bar-kitchenette et une terrasse. Il est construit à des hauteurs de 3,5 à 6 m au-dessus du sol pour une surface utile de 160 m² dont 65 en terrasse. La structure en mélèze, pin de Douglas et sapin repose sur des pilotis de bois. Les murs sont inclinés de 7°. Le coût total du projet s'est élevé à 350 000 € dont 200 000 d'honoraires pour le concepteur.

The ample scale and nature of this project sets it apart from most tree houses. It is set on wooden pillars, and existing trees on the site are allowed to grow through the wooden decking (right).

Die großzügigen Dimensionen und das Konzept des Projekts unterscheiden es von den meisten Baumhäusern. Der Bau ruht auf Holzstützen, Bäume auf dem Grundstück dürfen durch die Holzterrasse wachsen.

L'ampleur et la nature de ce projet lui confèrent une place à part. Il s'appuie sur des piliers de bois et les arbres ont conservé leur liberté (ci-contre).

The interiors are essentially finished in white and furniture blends with the style of the structure itself. Left page, a built-in seating area.

Das Interieur ist primär in Weiß gehalten, das Mobiliar harmoniert stilistisch mit dem Bau. Links im Bild eine Sitznische.

L'intérieur est essentiellement traité en blanc et le mobilier est harmonisé avec le style de la maison. À gauche une petite alcôve autour d'une table.

28

Designed by Casa na Árvore
Araras, São Paulo (Brazil)

lake house

Casa na Árvore is owned by Ricardo Brunelli, Brazil's leading builder of tree houses. Brunelli took an intern who had worked with Pete Nelson to build this tree house which is located on the grounds of a large lakeside estate. It is used for "relaxation and entertaining guests." The tree house is built in a grove of eucalyptus trees, one of which crosses through the living room, and with a number of subsidiary platforms and elevated walkways. A playroom for children at the edge of the main deck is part of the design. Mahogony and teak were used for parts of the structure.

Hausherr der Casa na Árvore ist Ricardo Brunelli, Brasiliens führender Baumhausgestalter. Brunelli lud einen ehemaligen Mitarbeiter von Pete Nelson in sein Baumhaus auf einem weitläufigen Seegrundstück ein. Der Bau dient „zur Entspannung und zum Empfang von Gästen" und wurde in einen Eukalyptushain gebaut. Einer der Bäume wächst durch den Wohnbereich. Das Haus umfasst verschiedene kleinere Terrassen und Brücken. Auch ein Spielzimmer für Kinder am Rande der Hauptterrasse wurde in den Entwurf integriert. Teile des Baus wurden in Mahagoni und Teak realisiert.

Casa na Árvore, propriété de Ricardo Brunelli, est le principal fabricant de maisons dans les arbres au Brésil. Brunelli emmena un stagiaire, qui avait travaillé avec Pete Nelson, visiter cette maison située dans un vaste domaine en bordure d'un lac. La maison est utilisée pour la détente ou recevoir des invités. Construite en acajou et teck dans un bosquet d'eucalyptus dont l'un traverse le séjour, elle présente un certain nombre de plates-formes et de passerelles. La petite salle de jeux pour les enfants à l'extrémité de la terrasse principale est un élément intéressant du projet.

Unlike many other tree houses, this structure is truly built around and supported by host trees. It blends into its setting well, but still has modern features, such as the triangular window seen below.

Anders als viele andere Baumhäuser wurde dieser Bau tatsächlich um Bäume herumgebaut und wird von ihnen getragen. Trotz moderner Details wie einem Dreiecksfenster (unten) fügt es sich harmonisch in sein Umfeld.

À la différence de nombreuses maisons dans les arbres, cette structure est réellement construite autour des arbres qui la soutiennent. Elle se fond bien dans son environnement, mais présente néanmoins des aspects modernes, comme la fenêtre triangulaire ci-dessous.

With the large eucalyptus trunk crossing through the living space, it is hard for the visitor to forget that one is in the trees here, even though the level of luxury is high.

Dank des mächtigen Eukalyptusstamms im Wohnraum vergisst der Besucher sicher nicht, dass er hoch in den Bäumen schwebt – trotz luxuriöser Ausstattung.

Face à cet énorme eucalyptus qui traverse le séjour, le visiteur ne peut oublier qu'il se trouve dans les arbres, même si les aménagements sont luxueux.

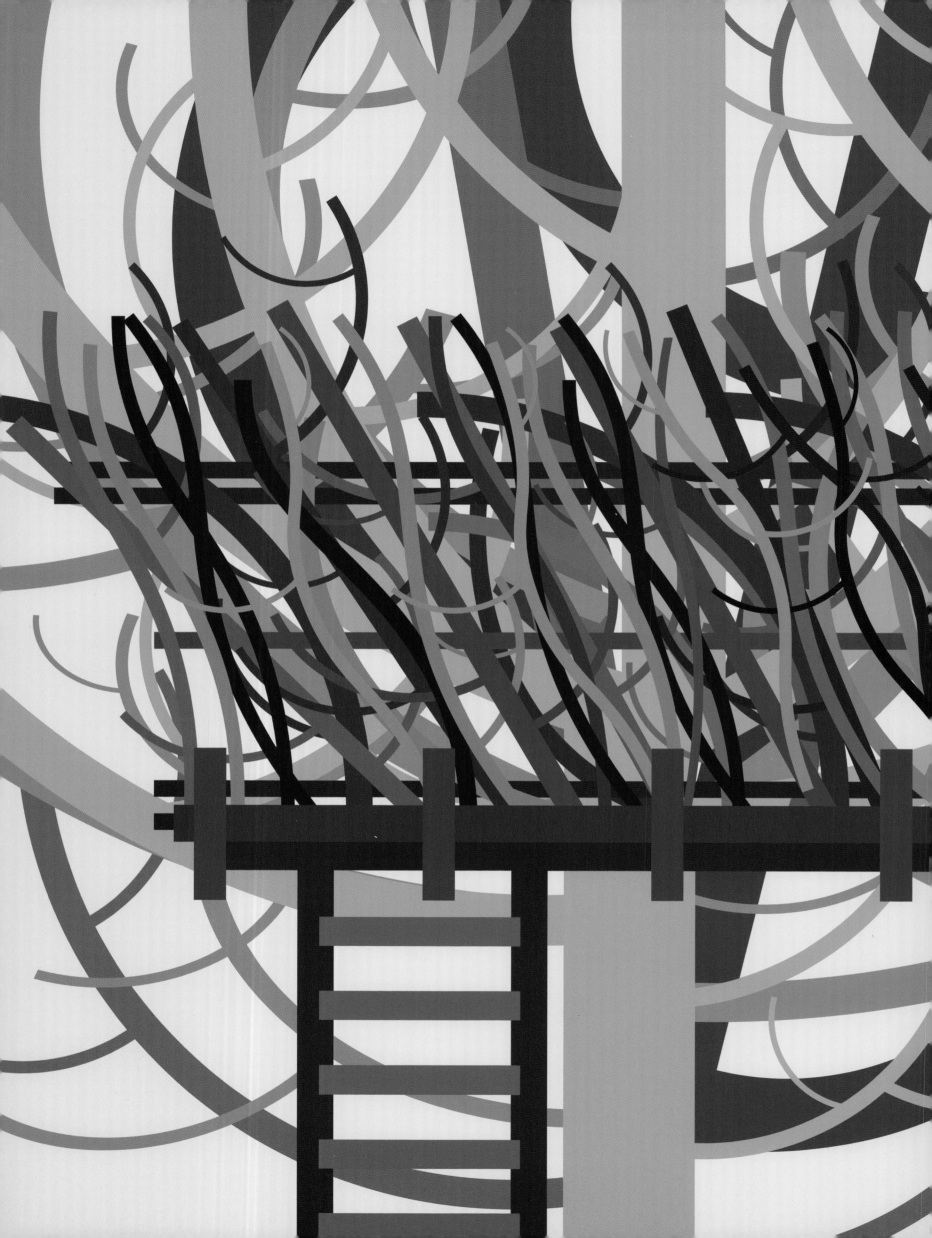

29

Designed by Roderick Wolgamott Romero
New York (USA) — 2009

lake-nest tree house

Roderick Wolgamott Romero collected driftwood along the shore of Long Island and obtained salvaged lumber from Antique and Vintage Woods of America. He explains: "The client wanted a place to read a book, to have the children up for adventures, and a beautiful spot for sunset cocktails." Two independent 18.6-square-meter structures are respectively located at heights of 6 and 10.7 meters above the ground. The tree house is intended to be almost completely invisible amongst the summer leaves.

Roderick Romero ergänzte das von ihm am Strand von Long Island gesammelte Treibholz mit zugekauftem Altholz von Antique and Vintage Woods of America. Romero berichtet: „Der Auftraggeber wollte einen Ort, um sich zurückziehen und ein Buch lesen zu können, für Abenteuerbesuche der Kinder und als Ort, an dem man bei Sonnenuntergang Cocktails trinken und die Aussicht genießen kann." Zwei unabhängige Module mit jeweils 18,6 m² wurden auf sechs beziehungsweise 10,7 m Höhe über dem Boden installiert. Im Sommer verschwindet das Baumhaus fast vollständig hinter dem Laub der Bäume.

Roderick Wolgamott Romero a ramassé du bois de mer le long de la côte de Long Island et trouvé du bois de récupération chez Antique and Vintage Woods of America : « Mon client souhaitait un lieu où pouvoir aller lire un livre, entraîner ses enfants dans un monde d'aventures et disposer d'un endroit magnifique pour prendre un cocktail au coucher du soleil. » Les deux structures indépendantes de 18,6 m² sont suspendues à respectivement 6 et 10,7 m du sol. Elles sont pratiquement invisibles, dès que le feuillage apparaît.

Though it might bring to mind the Bird's Nest Tree House (Harads Tree Hotel, p. 70) published in this volume, this double structure assumes a much more "natural" style and appearance. It seems to truly blend into its tree on two levels.

Trotz seiner Ähnlichkeit mit dem Bird's Nest Tree House in diesem Band (Tree Hotel in Harads, S. 70) wirkt dieses Baumhaus wesentlich „natürlicher". Mit seinen zwei Ebenen fügt es sich organisch in den tragenden Baum.

Bien qu'elle rappelle la Bird's Nest Tree House (Hardas Tree Hotel, p. 70) publiée dans cet ouvrage, cette double structure présente un aspect et un style beaucoup plus naturels. Ses deux niveaux semblent vraiment disparaître dans leur arbre.

The tree house is more a platform in the branches than it is an enclosed space, as is often the case of the structures in this book. It is as close to nature as it could be.

Das Baumhaus ist eher eine Plattform zwischen den Zweigen als ein umbauter Raum wie viele andere Bauten in diesem Band. Der Bau ist der Natur so nah, wie man es sich nur denken kann.

La maison est davantage une plate-forme dans les branches qu'un espace fermé. Elle est aussi proche de la nature que l'on puisse être.

30

**Designed by Enéa on the basis
of an idea by Kelber Rosilion for Dans mon Arbre**
Parc de l'An Mil, Château de Langeais (France) — 2008

langeais castle tree house

This is a play area located on the grounds of the Château de Langeais. It has 55 steps and six stairways, leading to six levels perched between 6.5 and 10 meters above ground level. The total floor area is 37 square meters. The tree house is built in a massive cedar of Lebanon. Branches were pierced according to their size, and one difficulty of the design was allowing for the branches to move independently. Larch was used for the exterior cladding of the structure, which cost a total of €77 000. Construction took place on a site that was not accessible to trucks.

Das Abenteuerbaumhaus auf dem Anwesen des Château de Langeais wird über 55 Stufen und sechs Treppen erschlossen. Es hat sechs Ebenen in 6,5 bis 10 m Höhe. Die Gesamtfläche beträgt 37 m². Das Baumhaus wurde aus massivem Zedernholz realisiert. Stämme und Äste wurden ihrer Größe entsprechend umbaut; eine Herausforderung des Entwurfs war, die freie Beweglichkeit der Äste zu gewährleisten. Der Außenbau der Konstruktion wurde mit Lärchenholz verkleidet, die Gesamtkosten des Projekts beliefen sich auf 77 000 €. Gebaut wurde an einem Standort, der nicht für Lieferfahrzeuge zugänglich ist.

Cette maison est située dans une aire de jeux du domaine du château de Langeais. Six escaliers et 55 marches donnent accès aux six niveaux perchés entre 6,5 et 10 m au-dessus du sol. La surface totale est de 37 m². La construction a été réalisée en cèdre du Liban massif. Les branches ont été percées et l'une des difficultés du projet était de leur permettre de se balancer indépendamment les unes des autres. L'habillage extérieur est en mélèze et l'ensemble a coûté 77 000 €. Le site de construction n'était pas accessible en camion.

With its rather complex structure and multi-level design, the Langeais Castle Tree House is, indeed, something of an exception in the realm of structures in the air.

Mit seiner komplexen Konstruktion und den zahlreichen Ebenen ist das Baumhaus am Château Langeais tatsächlich ein Sonderfall unter den schwebenden Bauten.

De structure assez complexe et de conception sur plusieurs niveaux, la maison de Langeais fait un peu figure d'exception dans sa catégorie.

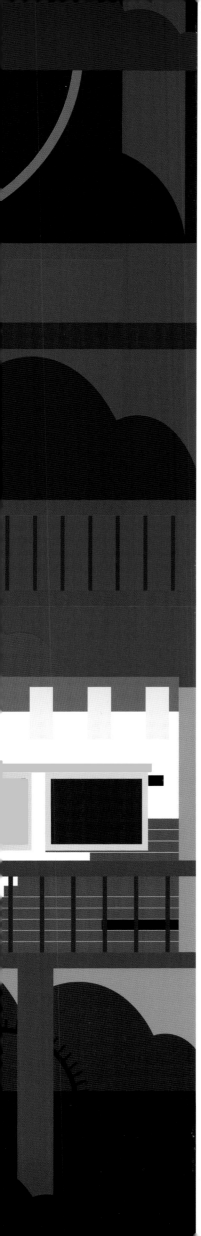

31

Designed by Les Nids
Le Locle, Neuchâtel (Switzerland)

les nids

The Nids (Nests) are small houses built in ash trees perched between five and eight meters above the earth in a forested area above the town of Le Locle. Le Locle is in the Jura area of Switzerland, a few kilometers from La Chaux-de-Fonds. There are independent "studios" for two to four people, with kitchenettes, shower, toilet, and heating. They can be acceded to by ramps and stairways. Two structures called La Sitelle and La Mésange are intended for two people, while Le Chouett'Nid and the Pic Epèche tree houses are reserved for families. The owners reserve the right to cancel reservations in the case of high winds. As they point out, these may be "nests" but the customers don't have wings!

Die kleinen Baumhausbauten Les Nids (Die Nester) schweben zwischen 5 und 8 Meter über dem Boden und liegen in einem Waldgebiet in der Nähe von Le Locle. Die Kleinstadt im Schweizer Jura liegt nur wenige Kilometer von La Chaux-de-Fonds entfernt. In den Baumhäusern sind eigenständige „Studios" für zwei bis vier Personen untergebracht, jeweils mit Kochzeile, Dusche, Toilette und Heizung. Erschlossen werden die Bauten über Rampen und Treppen. Die Häuser La Sitelle und La Mésange bieten Platz für zwei Personen, während Le Chouett'Nid und Pic Epèche für Familien eingerichtet wurden. Die Eigentümer behalten sich vor, Reservierungen bei starkem Wind zu stornieren. Auch wenn es sich um „Nester" handelt, so die Vermieter, können die Gäste doch leider nicht fliegen.

Les Nids sont de petites maisons perchées dans des frênes entre cinq et huit mètres au-dessus du sol au milieu d'une forêt près de la ville du Locle dans le Jura suisse, à quelques kilomètres de la Chaux-de-Fonds. Ce sont des « studios » indépendants conçus pour deux ou quatre personnes, équipés d'une cuisinette, d'une douche, de toilettes et d'un chauffage. On y accède par des rampes et des escaliers. La Sitelle et la Mésange accueillent les couples, le Chouett'Nid et le Pic Epêche les familles. Les propriétaires peuvent annuler les réservations si le vent est trop fort car si ces maisons sont des nids, « les clients n'ont pas d'ailes », font-ils remarquer.

Right page, the Mésange Tree House. Above, the Pic Epèche Tree House; left, a view from below showing the relatively simple design of a tree house supported by one trunk.

Auf der rechten Seite das Baumhaus La Mésange. Oben das Haus Pic Epèche, links ein Blick von unten auf die recht schlichte Konstruktion eines der Häuser, das auf einem einzelnen Baumstamm ruht.

Page de droite, la Mésange. Ci-dessus, le Pic Epèche. À gauche, vue en contre-plongée d'une maison relativement simple reposant sur un seul tronc.

On the right-hand side on top, the kitchen area of the Sitelle Tree House. Underneath, the interior of the Pic Epèche Tree House with its relatively generous space—bunk bed, kitchen, and wood stove. The structures have generous terraces that allow users to dine in the treetops.

Rechts oben der Küchenbereich im Haus Sitelle. Darunter ein Blick in das recht geräumige Baumhaus Pic Epèche – mit Etagenbett, Küche und Holzofen. Die Häuser haben großzügige Balkone, auf denen die Gäste unter Bäumen essen können.

À droite en haut, la cuisinette de la Sitelle. Dessous, l'intérieur du Pic Epèche, une maison relativement spacieuse (lits superposés, cuisine et poêle à bois). Les maisons disposent de généreuses terrasses qui permettent de dîner dans les arbres.

32

Designed by Andreas Wenning (baumraum)
Osnabrück (Germany) — 2009

magnolia
and fir

Located in dense bushes between a magnolia and several pine trees, this structure was intended as a guest space and playroom for a family's grandchildren, or as a retreat or meeting place for the owners. A stairway and a catwalk link a terrace and a closed cube-shaped space set on a brushed stainless-steel framework. Façades and the terrace are clad in tatajuba wood, while a reddish oak wood is used for the 13.6-square-meter interior. Built-in boxes for storage and light-gray upholstery increase the comfort level of the interior, as do a hi-fi system and a heater. With the terrace located three meters above the ground and the tree house itself at an altitude of four meters, the house has a pivoting window that offers a southern view of the Teutoburger Forest.

Das in dichtem Unterholz zwischen einer Magnolie und Tannen gelegene Baumhaus wurde als Gäste- und Spielzimmer für die Enkel der Familie geplant, sowie als Rückzugsort und Treffpunkt für das Bauherrenpaar. Terrasse und Kubus ruhen auf einem Rahmen aus gebürstetem Edelstahl und werden über eine Treppe und einen Steg erschlossen. Fassade und Terrasse wurden mit Tatajubaholz verblendet, während im 13,6 m² großen Innenraum rötliche Eiche zum Einsatz kam. Komfortabel wird das Interieur durch eingebaute Schubkästen, die Stauraum bieten, hellgraue Polsterelemente sowie eine Stereoanlage und Heizung. Die Terrasse in 3 m Höhe und das auf 4 m gelegene Baumhaus mit Kippfenstern bieten Ausblick nach Süden in den Teutoburger Wald.

Au milieu d'une dense végétation, posée entre un magnolia et quelques pins, cette maison sert à la fois de chambre d'amis, de salle de jeux pour enfants, de retraite et de lieu de réception pour ses propriétaires. Un escalier et une passerelle relient la terrasse à la maison en forme de cube, qui repose sur une ossature en acier inoxydable brossé. Les façades et la terrasse sont habillées de bois de tatajuba et les 13,6 m² de l'intérieur en chêne rouge. Des rangements et des sièges rembourrés gris clair comme un système hi-fi et un chauffage assurent un certain confort. La maison est suspendue à quatre mètres du sol et la terrasse à trois mètres. Une fenêtre pivotante offre une vue sur la forêt de Teutoburger Wald.

Rather than the curves he usually employs, in this instance Andreas
Wenning has chosen a strict boxlike form. Although built around trees,
it is supported by four metal pillars. A light staircase and intermediate
platform lead up to the tree house.

Statt der für ihn sonst typischen geschwungenen Formen entschied sich
Andreas Wenning hier für einen strengen Kubus. Die Konstruktion wurde
um einen Baum gebaut, wird jedoch von vier Metallstützen getragen.
Eine leichte Treppe und eine Zwischenebene führen zum Baumhaus
hinauf.

Au lieu des courbes qu'il préfère habituellement, Andreas Wenning a
choisi ici la forme rigoureuse de la boîte. Bien qu'elle soit construite
autour de quatre arbres, elle est également soutenue par quatre piliers
métalliques. Un escalier léger et une plate-forme intermédiaire conduisent à la maison.

Above, a view of the intermediate platform on the way up to the tree house. Right page, an interior view with a long band window, skylight, and built-in furnishings made with the usual high quality of baumraum.

Oben ein Blick auf die Zwischenebene auf dem Weg zum Baumhaus. Rechts ein Blick in den Innenraum mit einem langen Fensterband, Oberlicht und Einbauten in der für baumraum typischen hohen Qualität.

Ci-dessus, vue de la plate-forme intermédiaire de l'escalier de la maison. À droite, vue intérieure montrant la fenêtre en bandeau, la verrière et les meubles intégrés réalisés avec soin par l'équipe de baumraum.

33

Designed by Andreas Wenning (baumraum)
Lago di Bracciano, near Rome (Italy) — 2007

meditation tree house

Set four meters up in an old chestnut tree, this 14.6-square-meter tree house is supported by two supports and a set of steel cables and textile straps. A staircase leads up to a 16-square-meter terrace. The cubic structure is used by the client as a meditation space. Both the framework of the tree house and the terrace were built with untreated larch, while tropical tatajuba wood was used for the façade. White walls, oiled jatobá floors, a bench area, and cushions form the interior. A glassed roof, windows that run down to the floor of the tree house, and doors that can be opened fully allow for broad connections between the structure and its setting.

Das vier Meter hoch in eine Kastanie gebaute, 14,6 m² große Baumhaus wird von zwei Stützen und mehreren Stahlkabeln und Gurtschlaufen getragen. Eine Treppe führt hinauf zur Terrasse. Der kubische Bau wird von der Bauherrin als Meditationsraum genutzt. Rahmenkonstruktion und Terrasse des Baumhauses sind in unbehandelter Lärche gehalten, bei der Fassade kam Tatajuba-Tropenholz zum Einsatz. Der Innenraum wird von weißen Wänden, geölten Jatobá-Dielen, einer Bank und Kissen dominiert. Ein Dachfenster und geschosshohe Glastüren, die sich vollständig öffnen lassen, sorgen für eine enge Einbindung in das landschaftliche Umfeld.

Suspendue à quatre mètres de haut dans un vieux châtaignier, cette maison de 14,6 m² est soutenue par deux piliers et un ensemble de câbles d'acier et de sangles. Un escalier conduit à une terrasse de 16 m². Cette structure cubique est utilisée comme espace de méditation. L'ossature de la maison et de la terrasse est en mélèze non traité et la façade en bois tropical de tatajuba. L'intérieur aux murs blancs possède un sol en jatoba huilé et une banquette intégrée. La verrière zénithale, les baies toute hauteur et les portes coulissantes peuvent s'ouvrir entièrement pour offrir une connexion maximale entre l'intérieur et le cadre environnant.

This tree house is supported in part by its host tree but also by two wooden supports. The basic form of the structure is a cube. Generous glazing provides a close connection between the interior and exterior of the tree house.

Das Baumhaus wird teilweise vom Baum, zusätzlich jedoch von zwei Holzstützen getragen. Die Grundform des Baus ist kubisch. Dank großzügiger Verglasung ergibt sich eine enge Verknüpfung von Innen- und Außenraum.

La maison est supportée en partie par son arbre mais aussi par deux poteaux de bois. De forme essentiellement cubique, ses généreuses ouvertures créent un sentiment de proximité intérieur-extérieur.

With its skylight and sliding doors, the tree house looks more like a modern ground-level residence (right). The tree penetrates the outdoor terrace (below).

Mit seinem Oberlicht und den Schiebetüren wirkt das Baumhaus fast wie ein moderner Bungalow (rechts). Der Baum wächst durch die Außenterrasse (unten).

Équipée d'une verrière et de portes coulissantes, cette maison fait presque penser à un pavillon au sol (à droite). L'arbre traverse franchement la terrasse (ci-dessous).

34

Designed by Tham & Videgård Arkitekter
Harads (Sweden) — 2008–10

mirrorcube tree hotel

The Tree Hotel is located in the north of Sweden. The structure designed by Tham & Videgård is made in good part of lightweight aluminum. Hung around a tree, it is 4 x 4 x 4 meters in size and is clad in mirrored glass. Plywood is employed for the interiors and the tree house offers a 360° view of the forest surroundings. The structure allows for a double bed, bath, living room, and a roof terrace. Intended for two people, the tree house can be acceded to by a rope ladder or a rope bridge. Managed by a small nearby hotel called the Brittas Pensionat, the structure is meant as a prototype for at least 10 other similar tree-house hotel rooms.

Das Tree Hotel in Nordschweden, ein Entwurf von Tham & Videgård, wurde weitgehend mit Leichtaluminium realisiert. Die 4 x 4 x 4 m große Konstruktion hängt an einem Baum und ist mit Spiegelglas verkleidet. Beim Innenausbau des Baumhauses kamen Sperrholzplatten zum Einsatz. Von hier aus bietet sich ein 360°-Ausblick in die waldige Umgebung. Das Haus bietet Platz für Doppelbett, Küchenzeile, Bad, Wohnbereich und eine Dachterrasse. Das für zwei Personen geplante Baumhaus ist über eine Strickleiter oder Hängebrücke erreichbar. Der von Brittas Pensionat, einem kleinen Hotel in der Gegend, verwaltete Bau ist Prototyp für mindestens zehn weitere ähnliche Baumhaushotels.

Le Tree Hotel se trouve dans le nord de la Suède. Construit en grande partie en aluminium léger, il a été réalisé par Tham & Videgård. Suspendu au tronc d'un arbre il mesure 4 x 4 x 4 m et est habillé de verre-miroir. L'intérieur doublé de contreplaqué offre une vue à 360° sur la forêt environnante. La « maison » comprend un séjour, une terrasse sur le toit et est équipée d'un lit double, d'une kitchenette, et d'une salle d'eau. Conçue pour deux personnes, elle est accessible par une échelle de corde ou un pont de corde. Gérée par un petit hôtel voisin, le Brittas Pensionat, elle est le prototype d'une dizaine de chambres qui devraient ainsi se retrouver suspendues dans les arbres.

A light ramp leads up to the mirrored cubic tree house. Depending on the angle of view, the structure almost disappears into its forest background, and seems to hang in space.

Ein filigraner Steg führt zum verspiegelten Würfel-Baumhaus. Aus manchen Blickwinkeln verschmilzt der Bau geradezu mit der Waldkulisse und scheint in der Luft zu schweben.

Une passerelle légère conduit à la maison cubique et réfléchissante. Selon l'angle de vue, la structure disparaît presque dans son environnement de forêt, suspendue dans l'espace.

The bright interior of the hotel space contains living space, beds, and such features as electric heating. It allows views of the natural setting but remains a thoroughly modern and civilized environment.

Das helle Interieur des Hotelzimmers umfasst einen Wohnbereich, Betten und eine elektrische Heizung. Von hier aus hat man Ausblick in die Natur, das Umfeld jedoch ist uneingeschränkt modern und komfortabel.

L'intérieur lumineux contient un espace de séjour, des lits et quelques équipements dont un chauffage électrique. Les vues du cadre naturel sont omniprésentes, mais l'atmosphère reste moderne et civilisée.

In these images, taken at nightfall, the windows of the cube are visible, but otherwise its surface practically dissolves into the trees.

Auf diesen abendlichen Ansichten zeichnen sich die erleuchteten Fenster des Kubus ab, während die Spiegelflächen ansonsten mit den Bäumen zu verschmelzen scheinen.

Dans ces images, prises à la tombée de la nuit, la maison disparaît à l'exception des fenêtres, lorsqu'elle est occupée.

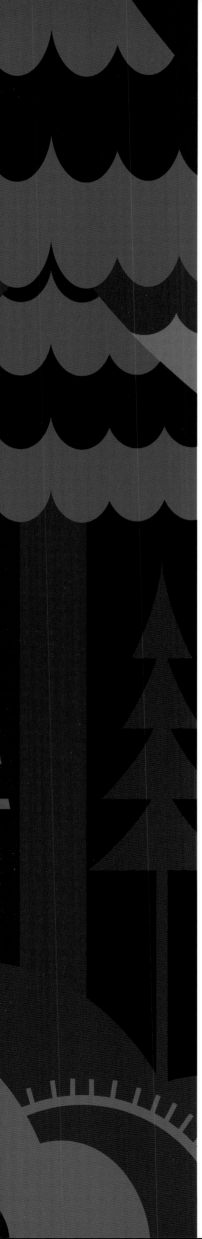

35

Designed by Nicko Bjorn Elliot
Toronta (Canada)

nicko bjorn elliot tree house

Designed as a children's play house, the structure wraps around a pine tree but is supported by three pilotis. Children can slide down a pole to exit. Translucent corrugated fiberglass cladding allows daylight in and makes the tree house glow from within at night. The architect explains: "Eight-year-old Joris and his big sister Matana, 10, sought a tree fort refuge on their downtown Toronto property to evoke the pleasures of the country cottage during busy summers in the city."

Das Kinderspielhaus wurde um eine Kiefer gebaut, wird jedoch von drei Pilotis getragen. Verlassen können die Kinder das Haus über eine Feuerwehrstange. Tageslicht erhält der Bau durch eine Verschalung mit lichtdurchlässigen Acryl-Wellplatten, dank derer das Haus nachts von innen leuchtet. Der Architekt schreibt: „Der achtjährige Joris und seine große Schwester Matana, zehn, wünschten sich auf ihrem Stadtgrundstück in Toronto eine Burg und ein Refugium in den Bäumen, das sie in Sommern in der Stadt an Ferien auf dem Land erinnert."

Conçue comme une maison-jouet pour enfants, cette structure englobe un pin mais repose néanmoins sur trois pilotis. Les enfants peuvent glisser le long d'un mât pour sortir. Les façades en fibre de verre ondulée translucide laissent entrer la lumière et créent un effet de lanterne pendant la nuit. « Joris, huit ans, et sa grande sœur Matana, dix ans, cherchaient un refuge dans les arbres dans la propriété de leurs parents au centre de Toronto, pour se rappeler les plaisirs de la campagne lors des étés passés en ville », explique l'architecte.

The tree house glows like a lantern from within at night (right page). The pole the children can slide down is visible in the image below on this page.

Nachts leuchtet das Baumhaus wie eine Laterne (rechte Seite). Unten im Bild die Feuerwehrstange, an der die Kinder hinunterrutschen können.

La nuit, la maison brille comme une lanterne (page de droite). Le mât utilisé par les enfants pour descendre est visible ci-dessous, sur cette page.

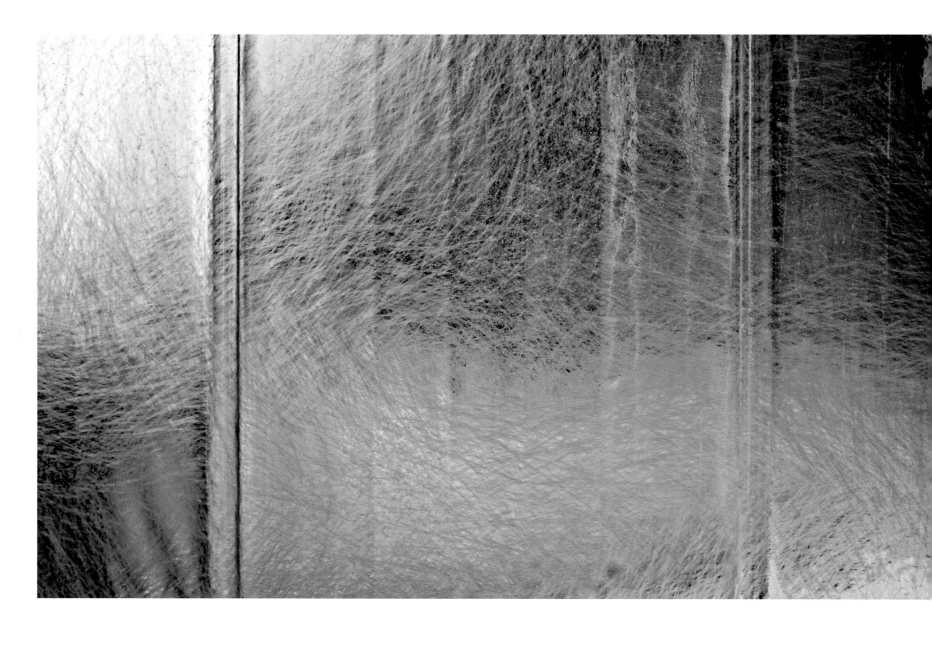

The translucent fiberglass skin of the house admits colors and shadows (above). The interior space is generous and open, with light penetrating from all sides. Wood and fiberglass are the only basic materials employed inside.

Die Verschalung des Hauses aus lichtdurchlässiger Glasfaser sorgt für Farb- und Schattenspiele (oben). Der Innenraum ist großzügig und offen, Licht fällt von allen Seiten ein. Die im Innern verbauten Grundmaterialien sind Holz und Glasfaser.

La peau translucide de la maison crée des effets d'ombres et de couleurs (page de droite). L'espace intérieur est ouvert et généreux, la lumière l'éclairant de tous côtés. Le bois et la fibre de verre sont les seuls matériaux employés à l'intérieur.

36

Designed by Andreas Wenning (baumraum)
Berlin (Germany) — 2010

on the spree

Located in the eastern part of Berlin, near a redeveloped port, this tree house is on the edge of the Spree River. It is attached with anchors and cables to a willow tree. As usual, Andreas Wenning employs thin tilted columns to support a good part of the weight of the tree house. The structure is covered in stainless-steel sheets cut with a laser. The interior can accommodate two or three people and includes a sofa and a working area. The white interiors include oak floors and fitted furniture.

Das im Osten Berlins realisierte Baumhaus liegt in der Nähe eines sanierten Hafenareals direkt am Ufer der Spree. Der Bau wurde mit Stahlkabeln in einer Weide verankert. Wie für ihn typisch, arbeitet Andreas Wenning auch hier mit schlanken schrägen Stützen, die einen Großteil der Lasten des Baumhauses ableiten. Der Bau wurde außen mit lasergeschnittenen Edelstahlplatten ummantelt. Der Innenraum mit Sofa und Arbeitsplatz bietet Platz für zwei bis drei Personen. Das weiße Interieur wurde mit Eichenboden und Einbaumöbeln ausgestattet.

Cette maison en bordure de la Spree se trouve dans la partie orientale de Berlin à proximité d'un port rénové. Elle est attachée par des câbles et des ancres à un saule. Comme d'habitude, Andreas Wenning a utilisé de fines colonnes d'acier pour soutenir une bonne partie du poids. La structure est habillée de tôle d'acier inoxydable découpée au laser. L'intérieur qui peut recevoir deux ou trois personnes comprend un sofa et un petit bureau. Équipé d'un mobilier, il est traité en blanc ; le sol est en chêne.

With its rounded forms and generous glazing, the Spree tree house looks almost as though it might move under its own power. In any case, it offers a privileged view of the river and the surroundings.

Aufgrund der gerundeten Form und großen Fenster könnte man das Baumhaus an der Spree fast für einen fahrbaren Untersatz halten. Es bietet eine unverwechselbare Aussicht auf Fluss und Umgebung.

De forme arrondie, généreusement ouverte, la maison semble presque capable de se déplacer d'elle-même. Elle offre une vue privilégiée sur la rivière et son environnement.

The white furniture is designed to form a continuous whole with the curving walls of the structure. The furnishings are edged with the same oak used on the floors.

Die weißen Einbauten wirken wie eine nahtlose Fortführung der geschwungenen Wandflächen und wurden mit Eiche abgesetzt. Auch der Boden wurde aus Eiche gefertigt.

Le mobilier blanc forme un tout continu avec les murs incurvés. Ses champs de coupe sont du même chêne que celui du plancher.

37

Designed by Andreas Wenning (baumraum)
Heilbronn (Germany) — 2005

pear
tree house

Built for an extended family with seven grandchildren, this four-meter-high tree house set in a large pear tree is on a property called "Äckerle" surrounded by orchards at the edge of the city of Heilbronn in northern Baden-Württemberg. A double spiral staircase and a terrace are attached to the pear tree by flexible textile hangers while the tree house itself is suspended in the tree using steel cables. Built with larch, the insulated tree house has an interior area of 8.6 square meters and also boasts a 12.4-square-meter terrace. Sunshades were used on the southwest to avoid excessive solar gain, while a glazed corner gives the bed area a view toward vineyards.

Das Baumhaus am Äckerle wurde für eine Großfamilie mit sieben Enkeln in vier Meter Höhe in einem großen Birnbaum realisiert. Es liegt inmitten von Obstgärten am Rande von Heilbronn im nördlichen Baden-Württemberg. Die doppelte Wendeltreppe und die Terrasse wurden mit flexiblen Gurtschlaufen am Birnbaum fixiert, während das eigentliche Baumhaus an Stahlkabeln hängt. Der gedämmte Bau aus Lärche hat eine Fläche von 8,6 m² sowie eine großzügige 12,4 m² große Terrasse. An der Südwestseite wurden Sonnenschutzblenden installiert, um die Sonneneinstrahlung zu reduzieren. Durch ein Eckfenster hat der Schlafbereich Blick auf die nahe gelegenen Weinberge.

Construite pour une grande famille comptant sept petits-enfants, cette maison dans les arbres de quatre mètres de haut a pris place dans un immense poirier sur une propriété appelée Äckerle entourée de vergers en limite de la ville de Heilbronn dans le nord du Bade-Wurtemberg. L'escalier en double spirale et la terrasse sont attachés au poirier par des suspentes souples en textile tandis que la maison elle-même est suspendue à l'arbre par des câbles d'acier. Construite en mélèze, elle offre une surface intérieure de 8,6 m² et une terrasse de 12,4 m². Au sud-ouest, des écrans protègent d'un gain solaire excessif et un angle vitré donne à la chambre une vue sur les vignobles.

The house is approached via a stairway and intermediate platform and has an elegant horizontal barrier that underlines the wooden forms. Anchored in the tree, the structure is also supported from the ground.

Das Haus wird über eine Treppe und eine Zwischenplattform erschlossen. Das elegante Geländer unterstreicht mit seinen Querstreben die Linienführung des Holzbaus, der nicht nur im Baum verankert wurde, sondern auch vom Boden gestützt wird.

On accède à la maison par un escalier à plate-forme intermédiaire dont l'élégant garde-corps met en valeur le dessin de la maison qui, accrochée à l'arbre, prend également appui sur le sol.

baumraum, Andreas Wenning   **262**

The smooth light wood interior contrasts with the stacked appearance of the stairs and platform (left page). Large openings and a skylight admit ample light and offer views of the setting.

Die nahtlosen, hellen Holzoberflächen des Interieurs kontrastieren mit der Schichtoptik von Treppe und Plattform (linke Seite). Große Fenster und ein Oberlicht lassen reichlich Tageslicht ins Haus und bieten Ausblick in die Gegend.

L'intérieur en bois poncé de couleur claire contraste avec la finition plus brute de l'escalier et de la plate-forme (page de gauche). De grandes baies et une verrière laissent pénétrer la lumière naturelle et offrent une vue sur le paysage.

38

Designed by Roderick Wolgamott Romero
New Mexico (USA) — 2006

petra cliff

This tree house was designed for the actor Val Kilmer. The client asked Roderick Wolgamott Romero to walk around his 2400-hectare property, the Pecos River Ranch, to find the ideal location for a tree house. Romero explains: "I spent five days walking, and walking and hiking … finally I found this amazing group of oak trees half way up a cliff … looking out over the Pecos River. The design was based on the nest made by the mud swallows that built their homes into the side of the cliffs." Using wood from an old dismantled barn, Romero created the structure that has 14 square meters of deck and an 11-square-meter interior.

Dieses Baumhaus wurde für den Schauspieler Val Kilmer geplant. Der Bauherr überließ es Roderick Romero, das 2400 ha große Anwesen zu erkunden, um den geeigneten Standort für ein Baumhaus zu finden. Romero erklärt: „Ich nahm mir fünf Tage Zeit, wanderte umher, wanderte und kletterte … und fand schließlich überraschend eine Gruppe von Eichen mitten an einem Steilabhang … mit Blick über den Pecos River. Für den Entwurf ließ ich mich von typischen Lehmnestern der Kliffschwalben inspirieren, die an Steilwänden nisten." Mit Altholz, Material vom Abriss einer Scheune, baute Romero ein Baumhaus mit einer 14 m² großen Terrasse und einem 11 m² großen Innenraum.

Cette maison dans l'arbre a été réalisée pour l'acteur américain Val Kilmer qui avait demandé à Roderick Romero de parcourir son domaine de 2400 ha, le Pecos River Ranch, pour trouver l'endroit idéal pour une maison dans les arbres. « J'ai passé cinq jours à marcher, marcher et grimper », explique Romero, « pour finalement trouver cet étonnant bosquet de chênes à mi-pente d'une falaise … donnant au loin sur la Pecos River. Le projet est inspiré des hirondelles à front blanc qui construisent leur nid dans les falaises. » En utilisant du bois récupéré dans une vieille grange démantelée, Romero a pu créer cette petite maison de 11 m² à terrasse de 14 m².

Built among oak trees on a cliff overlooking the river, this tree house has
a rustic appearance, almost as though it were a very old structure.

Das rustikale Baumhaus wirkt fast wie ein altes Haus und wurde
zwischen Eichen an einem Steilhang mit Blick über den Fluss gebaut.

Édifiée parmi les chênes d'une falaise donnant sur une rivière, cette
maison a l'air rustique, presque très ancienne.

Interiors and terraces use found wood and unfinished elements that confirm the rustic appearance of the exterior, and yet the whole is the product of sophisticated design.

Innenausbau und Terrassen wurden aus gefundenem Holz und unbehandelten Materialien gebaut, eine Optik, die dem rustikalen Außenbau entspricht. Dennoch ist das Haus das Ergebnis sorgfältiger Planung.

L'intérieur et la terrasse sont en bois trouvé et éléments bruts qui appuient l'aspect rustique de l'extérieur. L'ensemble n'en est pas moins le fruit d'une conception sophistiquée.

39

Designed by Go Hasegawa
Kita-Karuizawa, Gunma (Japan) — 2010

pilotis
in a forest

This 77-square-meter structure was designed with the intention to allow its owners and visitors to see the trunks of neighboring trees even when they are in the bottom section of the structure. Since this large lower space is entirely open, the architect explains: "I used the forest as the building's walls." He compares the suspended living area to a "small attic-like space" where a 1.8-meter ceiling and a low dining table sitting on a glass floor seek to "convey the sense that the natural environment outside is larger and closer."

Der 77 m² große Bau wurde so angelegt, dass Bauherren und Gäste Blick auf die Bäume des angrenzenden Waldstücks haben, selbst in der Zone unterhalb des Hauses. Diese untere Zone ist vollkommen offen gehalten, Grund für den Architekten zu erklären: „Ich habe den Wald als Wand interpretiert." Den darüber schwebenden Wohnbereich beschreibt er als „kleinen Raum, wie einen Dachboden". Die 1,8 m hohen Decken und ein niedriger Esstisch über einem gläsernen Bodeneinsatz „lassen den landschaftlichen Außenraum größer wirken und näher rücken".

Cette maison de 77 m² a été conçue pour que ses propriétaires et ses visiteurs puissent profiter de l'environnement boisé même dans sa partie inférieure. Ce grand espace au ras du sol est entièrement ouvert : « J'ai fait des arbres les murs de la maison », explique l'architecte. Il compare la partie suspendue à un « petit espace, comme un grenier » dont le plafond à 1,80 m de haut et la table des repas posée sur un sol de verre cherchent à « exprimer l'idée que l'environnement naturel extérieur est plus vaste et plus proche ».

The structure is lifted entirely off the ground and is reached by a suspended stairway. The space beneath this unusual tree house is also considered part of its usable area.

Der vollständig über dem Boden aufgeständerte Bau wird über eine abgehängte Treppe erschlossen. Auch die Zone unterhalb dieses ungewöhnlichen Baumhauses ist Teil der Nutzfläche.

La structure, accessible par un escalier suspendu, est entièrement soulevée au-dessus du sol. L'espace inférieur fait partie de la surface utile.

Both in the upper volume (above) and beneath the Pilotis in a Forest residents are in direct contact with nature, well away from the dense Japanese urban environment.

Sowohl im oberen Teil des Hauses (oben) als auch unterhalb des Pilotis-in-a-Forest-Refugiums haben die Bewohner direkten Kontakt zur Natur, fernab der dicht besiedelten japanischen Ballungsräume.

Dans le volume supérieur (ci-dessus) comme dans celui délimité par les pilotis, les résidents sont en contact direct avec la nature, loin de la densité du cadre urbain japonais.

The upper, suspended level of the structure provides for comfortable conditions quite literally in the midst of the natural setting of the forest.

Der obere, aufgeständerte Bereich des Hauses bietet komfortable Wohnbedingungen, und dies buchstäblich mitten im Wald.

Le niveau suspendu offre des conditions de vie confortables au cœur du cadre naturel de la forêt.

40

Designed by Andreas Wenning (baumraum)
Prague (Czech Republic) — 2009

prague tree house

Built in an oak tree on a property near the Czech capital, this tree house is for a family with two children. It has two terraces located respectively 3.5 and 4.5 meters above the ground. The actual tree house has a square plan. Cylindrical steel supports are used to complement the ropes and belt loops that hold up the terraces and part of the weight of the cabin. Large windows mark the interior, where oiled oak is used. The exteriors are in untreated larch, which, of course, ages well. A skylight adds to the exterior views provided in the Prague Tree House.

Das in eine Eiche gebaute Baumhaus auf einem Grundstück unweit der tschechischen Hauptstadt wurde für eine Familie mit zwei Kindern geplant. Seine zwei Terrassen liegen 3,5 und 4,5 m über dem Boden. Das Baumhaus selbst hat einen quadratischen Grundriss. Runde Stahlstützen ergänzen das System aus Seilen und Gurtschlaufen, das Terrassen und einen Teil der Lasten der Wohnkabine trägt. Große Fenster dominieren den Innenraum, in dem geölte Eiche verbaut wurde. Der Außenbau wurde aus unbehandeltem Lärchenholz realisiert, das besonders altersbeständig ist. Ein Dachfenster im Prager Baumhaus bietet eine zusätzliche Sichtachse nach außen.

Construite dans un chêne sur une propriété non loin de la capitale tchèque, cette maison a été conçue pour une famille et ses deux enfants. Elle possède deux terrasses, respectivement à 3,5 et 4,5 m du sol. Le plan de la maison est carré. Des supports en tube d'acier complètent les cordages et les sangles qui maintiennent les terrasses et supportent une partie du poids. L'intérieur en chêne huilé bénéficie de grandes fenêtres. L'extérieur est en hêtre non traité qui se patinera bien. Une verrière zénithale complète la diversité des vues de cette maison.

A tilted ladder leads up to the two successive terraces. The steel columns that support part of the weight of the cabin are visible on the right page.

Eine schräge Leiter führt hinauf zu den beiden übereinander-liegenden Terrassen. Rechts im Bild die Stahlstützen, die eine Teillast der Kabine ableiten.

Une échelle conduit aux deux terrasses successives. Les colonnes d'acier qui soutiennent une partie du poids de la maison sont visibles sur la page de droite.

baumraum, Andreas Wenning   **282**

Open and comfortable, the Prague Tree House has modern and sophisticated forms while fitting in very well with the idea that children might have of a tree house. The oak tree it is situated in was chosen because of its solidity.

Das Prager Baumhaus ist offen und komfortabel. Trotz der modernen, hochwertigen Formensprache entspricht es deutlich kindlichen Vorstellungen von einem Baumhaus. Die Eiche, in die es gebaut wurde, bot sich wegen ihrer Stabilität an.

Ouverte et confortable, la maison de Prague est d'aménagement moderne et sophistiqué tout en restant fidèle à l'idée que des enfants peuvent se faire d'un refuge dans les arbres. Le chêne a été choisi pour sa solidité.

41

Designed by Pete Nelson
Issaquah, Washington (USA)

sarah's tree house

Built between four Douglas fir trees and a maple, Sarah's Tree House includes such features as a hot tub and a zip line. According to Pete Nelson, the design, originally intended for card games or as a changing area for the hot tub, became the home office of the owner. A loft bed and television complement the already comfortable interior. Indeed, with its desktop computer, Sarah's Tree House has all the amenities of a small residence. Even its appearance brings to mind a small "normal" house that might somehow happen to be floating between the trees.

Sarahs Baumhaus wurde zwischen vier Douglaskiefern und einen Ahorn gebaut, zu den besonderen Highlights zählen ein Whirlpool und eine Seilrutsche. Laut Pete Nelson war der Entwurf ursprünglich als Ort zum Kartenspielen und Umkleidebereich für den Whirlpool geplant, wurde von der Bauherrin aber schließlich als privates Büro genutzt. Hochbett und Fernseher vervollständigen die ohnehin komfortable Einrichtung. Mit seinem Computeranschluss entspricht Sarahs Baumhaus tatsächlich dem Standard einer kleinen Wohnung. Auch von außen erinnert es an ein kleines „normales" Häuschen, das allerdings zwischen den Bäumen schwebt.

Construite entre quatre pins de Douglas et un érable, la maison dans les arbres de Sarah possède un jacuzzi et une tyrolienne. Selon Pete Nelson, le projet prévu à l'origine pour jouer aux cartes ou servir de vestiaire au jacuzzi est devenu le bureau de sa propriétaire. Un canapé et une télévision complètent ces aménagements confortables. Équipée d'un ordinateur, cette maison offre tous les services d'une petite résidence. Son apparence même fait penser à une maison « normale » qui aurait décidé d'aller flotter parmi les arbres.

Opposite page, an overall view of Sarah's Tree House. On this page, a platform leads to the zip line and (below) stairs lead down to the hot tub.

Auf der gegenüberliegenden Seite ein Blick auf Sarahs Baumhaus. Auf dieser Seite die Plattform, die zur Seilrutsche führt, sowie die Treppe zum Whirlpool (unten).

Page de droite, vue d'ensemble de la maison. Ci-contre, vue de la plate-forme d'où part la tyrolienne et ci-dessous, les escaliers qui conduisent au jacuzzi.

The interior, with its working space, computer, television, and loft bed has almost everything that makes a home away from home, a working refuge in the trees, with a hot tub for relaxation and a zip line for a quick escape.

Innen bietet das Haus mit einem Arbeitsplatz, Computer, Fernseher und einem Hochbett alles, was ein Ferienhaus braucht: ein Zufluchtsort in den Bäumen, mit einem Whirlpool zum Entspannen und einer Seilrutsche für kleine Fluchten.

L'intérieur (bureau, ordinateur, télévision et canapé) offre tout ce qui compose une petite résidence secondaire ou un refuge pour travailler dans les arbres, sans oublier le jacuzzi et la tyrolienne pour s'échapper.

42

Designed by Pete Nelson
Western New Jersey (USA)

solace
tree house

A maker of rustic furniture and an author, Dan Mack has worked for the client of this house in New Jersey for a number of years. The tree-house designer Pete Nelson writes that he has been "creating all kinds of whimsical structures, both large and small, on this weekend property." Built in a large sycamore tree, with the help of Nelson and his TreeHouse and Supply firm, the Solace Tree House has generous proportions and such unexpected features as walls covered in old newspapers. Designed in what Mack calls a "hobo style," the structure features a window-washer's chair that can be maneuvered up and down with an electric winch.

Dan Mack, Autor und Designer rustikaler Möbel, arbeitete über mehrere Jahre für den Bauherrn dieses Projekts in New Jersey. Baumhausarchitekt Pete Nelson zufolge realisierte Mack bereits „eine ganze Reihe fantasievoller Bauten, große wie kleine, auf diesem Wochenendgrundstück". Das Solace Tree House, mit Unterstützung von Nelson und seiner Firma TreeHouse and Supply in eine amerikanische Platane gebaut, ist großzügig geschnitten. Ungewöhnlich sind unter anderem die mit alten Zeitungen tapezierten Wände. Das Haus im „Bohème-Stil", so Mack, ist unter anderem mit einem Fensterlift ausgestattet, der sich mit einer elektrischen Winde auf- und abfahren lässt.

Fabricant de mobilier rustique et auteur, Dan Mack travaille pour le client de cette maison dans le New Jersey depuis plusieurs années. Le concepteur de maisons dans les arbres Pete Nelson écrit qu'il « a créé toutes sortes de constructions bizarres, grandes et petites, sur cette propriété de week-end ». Édifiée dans un grand sycomore, avec l'aide de Nelson et de son entreprise TreeHouse and Supply, cette maison de généreuses proportions multiplie les détails inattendus comme des murs tapissés de vieux journaux. Conçu dans un « style hobo », elle est dotée d'une chaise de laveur de carreaux qui peut être montée et descendue par un treuil électrique.

Entirely supported by the sycamore tree in which it is built, the Solace Tree House has struts holding the floor, generous glazing, and a surprising, ad hoc appearance that its designer calls a "hobo" style.

Das Solace Tree House wird vollständig von der amerikanischen Platane getragen, in die es gebaut ist, hat Druckstreben, die den Boden stützen und ist großzügig verglast. Das eklektische Erscheinungsbild bezeichnet der Planer als „Bohème-Stil".

Entièrement supportée par le sycomore, la maison repose néanmoins sur des tasseaux appuyés sur le tronc. Elle possède de grandes ouvertures vitrées et un aspect particulier, qualifié de « style hobo ».

The interior of the tree house has a decidedly rustic appearance, as evidenced by these views of the high-ceilinged living space. This style matches the exterior of the structure perfectly.

Innen wirkt das Haus betont rustikal, wie die Ansichten des hohen Wohnbereichs belegen. Stilistisch eine konsequente Fortführung des Außenbaus.

L'intérieur est décidément rustique comme le montrent ces vues du séjour à haut plafond, au style en accord avec celui de l'extérieur.

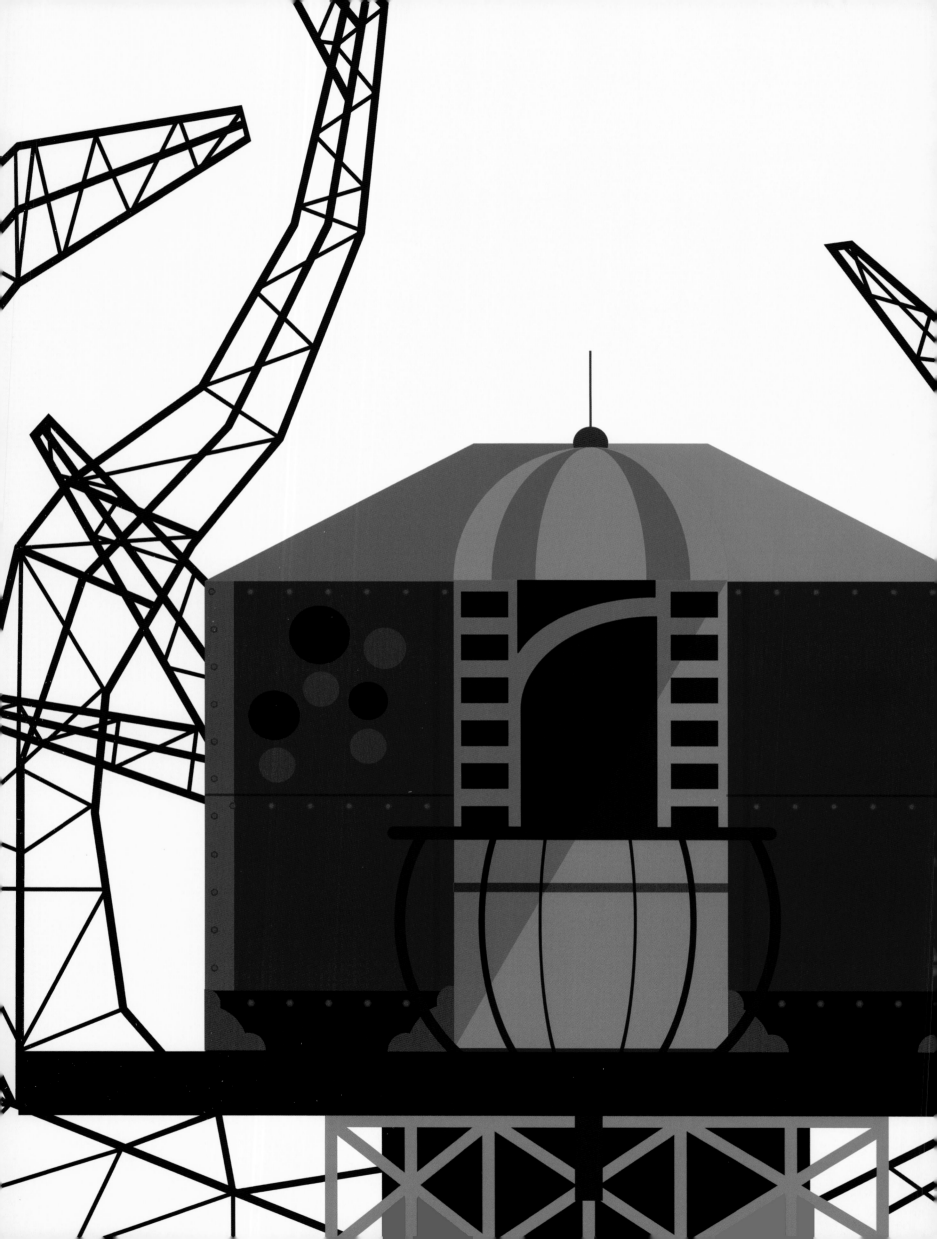

43

Designed by Sean Orlando and the Five Ton Crane Arts Group
Milton, Delaware (USA) — 2007

steampunk tree house

This unusual structure is described by its present owners, the Dogfish Head Craft Brewery, as "our off-centered, retro-futuristic sculpture." The work was designed by Sean Orlando and the Five Ton Crane Arts Group for the 2007 Burning Man festival in Black Rock City, Nevada. The structure is 12.2 meters high and just as wide. It weighs eight tons and was made with recycled and reclaimed materials. Sean Orlando explains that "the Steampunk Tree House was made to explore the relationship between our rapidly changing natural world and the persistent human drive to connect with it and one another. It is our second nature." Certainly not a tree house in the traditional sense, the Steampunk Tree House is nonetheless related to the genre.

Der heutige Besitzer, die Brauerei Dogfish Head Craft, nennt den ungewöhnlichen Bau eine „exzentrische, retro-futuristische Skulptur". Der Entwurf von Sean Orlando entstand in Zusammenarbeit mit der Five Ton Crane Arts Group für das Burning Man Festival 2007 in Black Rock City, Nevada. Der Bau ist 12,2 m hoch und ebenso breit. Die acht Tonnen schwere Konstruktion wurde aus Recycling- und Altmaterialien gebaut. Orlando zufolge entstand das „Steampunk Tree House als Auseinandersetzung mit unserer sich rasend verändernden Umwelt und dem unverbrüchlichen menschlichen Bedürfnis, den Kontakt zur Natur und zueinander zu suchen. Das ist unser natürlicher Instinkt." Das Steampunk Treehouse ist sicherlich kein Baumhaus im üblichen Sinne, aber dennoch diesem Genre zuzurechnen.

Cette curieuse construction est présentée par son propriétaire actuel, la Dogfish Head Craft Brewery, comme « notre sculpture rétro-futuriste décalée ». Conçue par Sean Orlando et le Five Ton Crane Arts Group pour le festival du Burning Man 2007 à Black Rock City dans le Nevada, elle mesure 12,2 m de haut pour une largeur similaire. Elle pèse huit tonnes et a été réalisée en matériaux recyclés ou récupérés. Sean Orlando explique que cette maison dans l'arbre « a été réalisée pour explorer les relations entre notre monde naturel en changement rapide et la tendance humaine persistante à s'y connecter. C'est notre seconde nature.» Certainement pas une maison dans les arbres au sens traditionnel, elle ne s'en rattache pas moins par ses branches à cette catégorie…

The Steampunk Tree House is unusual in that it is entirely artificial—a kind of mechanical tree house made with odd bits and pieces of metal.

Das Steampunk Tree House ist schon deshalb ungewöhnlich, weil es vollkommen künstlich ist – eine Art mechanisches Baumhaus aus Altmetallteilen.

La Steampunk Tree House est étonnante au sens où elle est entièrement artificielle, sorte de maison mécanique faite de morceaux de métal.

Sean Orlando and the Five Ton Crane Arts Group   **300**

The interior of the tree house has a "Jules Verne" kind of feeling to it—something out of an old science-fiction movie perhaps. Like many tree houses, it employs a vocabulary inspired by ship design.

Der Innenraum des Baumhauses hat eine gewisse „Jules-Verne-Nostalgie" und wirkt fast wie aus einem alten Sciencefiction-Film. Wie bei vielen Baumhäusern finden sich auch hier Stilelemente aus dem Bootsbau.

L'intérieur est traité dans un esprit à la Jules Verne ou dans l'esprit d'un vieux film de science-fiction. Comme souvent dans ce type de maisons, l'aménagement est inspiré de celui des bateaux.

takasugi-an

Takasugi-an means "a teahouse (built) too high." It is built between the trunks of two chestnut trees and is reached by ladders that are propped up against the trunks, which were cut and brought from a nearby site. A window in the teahouse frames a view of the town where the architect grew up. Because of its intimate dimensions, the teahouse takes on a personal aspect that is reinforced here by the fact that Professor Fujimori built the structure for himself on land belonging to his family. The interior space of the teahouse measures just 2.69 square meters, and although it does fit within the traditional constraints of the genre, Fujimori has taken some delight in creating the most eccentric or unexpected version of the genre.

Takasugi-an bedeutet so viel wie „Teehaus, zu hoch (gebaut)". Das Haus wurde zwischen zwei Kastanienstämme gebaut und ist über zwei Leitern zugänglich. Diese lehnen an den beiden Stämmen, die in der Nähe gefällt und an den Bauplatz transportiert wurden. Ein Fenster im Teehaus rahmt den Blick auf die Stadt, wo der Architekt seine Kindheit verbrachte. Durch die intime Größe gewinnt das Teehaus etwas Persönliches, und tatsächlich baute Professor Fujimori das Haus für sich selbst auf einem Grundstück der Familie. Der Innenraum des Teehauses misst lediglich 2,69 m² und obwohl es alle traditionellen Elemente des Genres aufweist, ließ sich Fujimori nicht das Vergnügen nehmen, eine denkbar exzentrische und überraschende Version zu realisieren.

Takasugi-an signifie « maison de thé trop haute ». Elle a été construite entre les troncs de deux marronniers coupés sur un terrain voisin et dressés sur place. On y accède par des échelles posées contre les troncs. Une fenêtre cadre une vue sur la ville où l'architecte a grandi. De par ses dimensions intimistes, cette maison de thé possède un aspect très personnel renforcé par le fait que Fujimori l'a construite pour lui-même sur un terrain appartenant à sa famille. L'espace intérieur ne mesure que 2,69 m² et bien qu'elle s'inscrive dans les contraintes traditionnelles du genre, l'architecte a pris un certain plaisir à créer la plus excentrique des maisons dans les arbres.

The roof of the tree house is covered in hand-rolled copper sheets.
The architect says he "is not interested in making a tree house on top
of a natural tree," preferring an "artificial construction."

Das Dach des Teehauses wurde mit handgerollten Kupferblechen
gedeckt. Der Architekt erklärt, er sei „nicht daran interessiert, ein Baumhaus in einen natürlichen Baum zu setzen", sondern interessiere sich
vielmehr für „künstliche Konstruktionen".

Le toit de la maison est en cuivre façonné à la main. L'architecte a
déclaré « ne pas être intéressé par une maison dans un arbre naturel »,
préférant « une construction artificielle ».

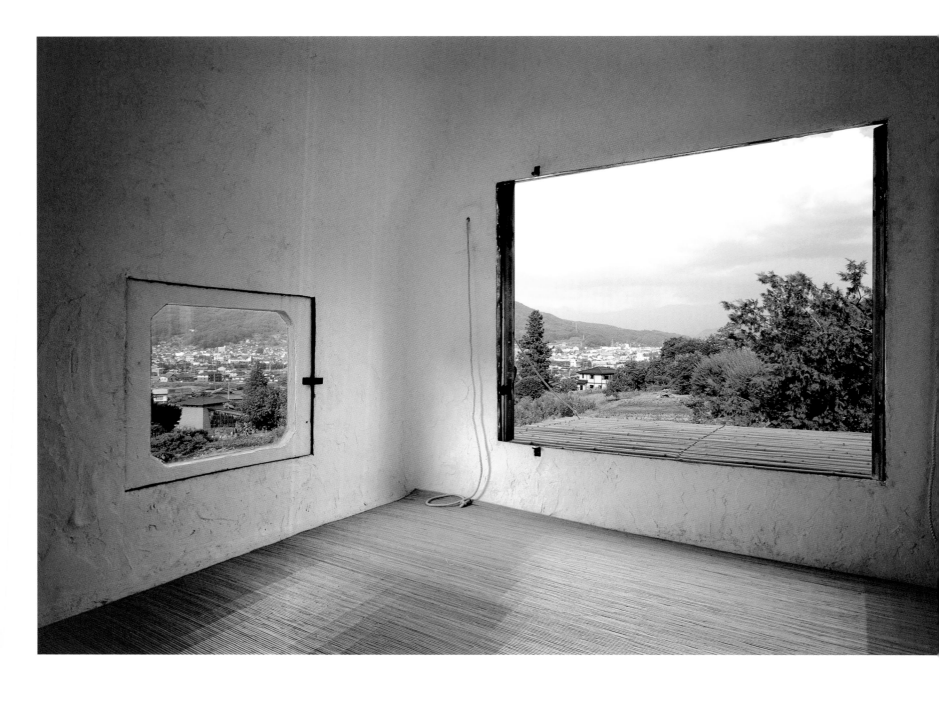

The architect placed a bamboo lattice outside the window seen here to reflect moonlight into the space at night. A small open hearth is used to make tea.

Der Architekt platzierte ein Bambusgitter vor dem Fenster, das nachts das Mondlicht in den Raum reflektiert. Eine kleine offene Feuerstelle dient zum Teekochen.

L'architecte a disposé un lattis de bambou devant une fenêtre pour refléter la lumière de la lune vers l'intérieur. Une petite cheminée sert à préparer le thé.

45

Designed by Terunobu Fujimori
Kiyoharu Shirakaba Museum, Nakamaru, Hokuto City, Yamanashi (Japan) — 2005

teahouse tetsu

"The site is famous for cherry blossoms…. When I go to see the cherry blossoms at night, it is as if I strayed into a dream world," says Terunobu Fujimori. "I did not intend it this way, but it looks as if it were a house for a midget from a fairy tale." Approached to build a teahouse on the grounds of the Kiyoharu Shirakaba Museum, Fujimori built this odd wooden structure next to a restaurant designed by Yoshio Taniguchi. Unlike traditional teahouses that are more inward looking, this one was designed to view cherry blossoms.

„Dieser Ort ist berühmt für seine Kirschblüte […]. Wenn ich abends hierher komme, um die Kirschblüte zu bewundern, ist es, als tauche man in eine Traumwelt ein", erzählt Terunobu Fujimori. „Ganz unbeabsichtigt wirkt das Haus wie ein Zwergenhaus aus einem Märchen." Fujimori hatte den Auftrag erhalten, ein Teehaus auf dem Areal des Kiyoharu-Shirakaba-Museums zu bauen und realisierte dieses ungewöhnliche Holzhaus neben einem Restaurant von Yoshio Taniguchi. Anders als traditionelle Teehäuser, die eher nach innen gewandt sind, wurde dieses für das Betrachten der Kirschblüte geplant.

« Ce site est fameux pour ses cerisiers en fleurs… Lorsque je vais regarder les cerisiers la nuit, c'est comme si je me glissais dans un monde de rêves », explique Terunobu Fujimori. « Ce n'était pas mon intention, mais elle fait penser à la maison des nains dans un conte de fées. » Contacté pour réaliser une maison de thé sur le terrain du musée Kiyoharu Shirakaba, Fujimori a construit cette structure en bois près d'un restaurant conçu par Yoshio Taniguchi. À la différence des maisons de thé traditionnelles, plus introverties, celle-ci a été spécifiquement conçue pour contempler les cerisiers en fleurs.

Supported by a single cypress trunk that passes through the structure, the teahouse is designed to sway with its support in case of storms or earthquakes.

Das Teehaus ruht auf einem Zypressenstamm, der sich durch den Bau zieht. Bei der Planung wurde berücksichtigt, dass der Bau bei Stürmen oder Erdbeben mit dem Stamm mitschwingen kann..

Soutenue par un unique tronc de cyprès qui la traverse, la maison de thé a été étudiée pour se balancer avec son support en cas de tempête ou de tremblement de terre.

The branches of the Japanese cypress tree trunk that supports the structure are visible in the interior space. Guests are meant to sit on the left of the space seen above.

Die Stämme der japanischen Zypresse, auf denen der Bau ruht, sind im Innenraum sichtbar. Gäste sitzen links vom Raum oben im Bild.

Les branches du cyprès japonais qui soutient la structure sont visibles de l'intérieur. Les hôtes s'assoient dans la partie gauche de l'espace ci-dessus.

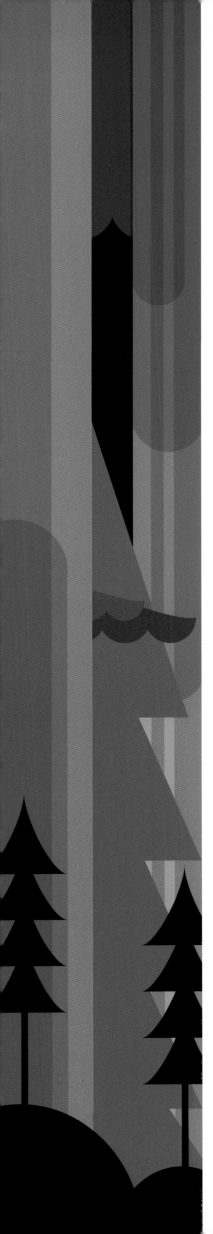

46

Designed by Pete Nelson
Issaquah, Washington (USA) — 2006

temple of
the blue moon

Part of Tree House Point, a complex intended to promote "a vision of sustainability while providing opportunities for lodging, education, and connection in a unique and natural environment," the Temple of the Blue Moon is a 23-square-meter structure built nearly five meters off the ground. Lodged between an ancient Sitka spruce and a western red cedar, the Temple of the Blue Moon was inspired by the form of the Parthenon. Available for rent, the structure has leather reading chairs, a writing desk, bookcase, and armoire, as well as a large bed.

Das 23 m² große Baumhaus Temple of the Blue Moon wurde rund 5 m über dem Boden gebaut und gehört zum Tree House Point, einem Projekt, das sich auf die Fahnen geschrieben hat, eine „Vision von Nachhaltigkeit" zu vermitteln und dabei „Unterkünfte, Bildungsangebote und ein einzigartiges Naturumfeld" anzubieten. Das zwischen einer alten Sitka-Fichte und einer Riesen-Thuja gebaute Baumhaus greift die Giebelform des Parthenon auf. Das Baumhaus, das gemietet werden kann, ist mit Ledersesseln, einem Schreibtisch, Regal, Kleiderschrank und einem großen Bett ausgestattet.

Faisant partie de Tree House Point, complexe dédié à la promotion d'une « vision de la durabilité tout en offrant des possibilités de logement, d'éducation et de contacts avec un environnement naturel exceptionnel », le Temple de la lune bleue est une construction de 23 m² édifiée à près de cinq mètres au-dessus du sol. Installé entre un très vieux sapin de Sitka et un cèdre rouge, le temple s'est inspiré du plan du Parthénon. Proposé à la location, il est équipé de sièges de lecture en cuir, d'un bureau, d'une bibliothèque, d'une armoire et d'un grand lit.

This project has an unusual mixture of what might be called rustic and classical qualities. The tree that pierces the structure supports it entirely.

Auffällig an diesem Projekt ist die ungewöhnliche Mischung rustikaler und klassischer Stilelemente. Das Haus wird vollständig vom Baum getragen, der es durchbohrt.

Ce projet est un étrange mélange de détails classiques et rustiques. La construction est exclusivement portée par le tronc central.

Rather luxurious in appearance with electric lighting in evidence here, the interiors offer views into the surrounding trees and the generous ceiling height of a house that might have remained firmly planted in the ground.

Das recht luxuriöse Interieur verfügt über elektrisches Licht, wie hier zu sehen. Von hier aus bietet sich Ausblick in die umstehenden Bäume. Die großzügige Deckenhöhe entspricht einem Haus zu ebener Erde.

D'aspect assez luxueux, l'intérieur équipé de l'éclairage électrique offre des vues sur les arbres environnants et la hauteur de plafond d'une résidence terrestre.

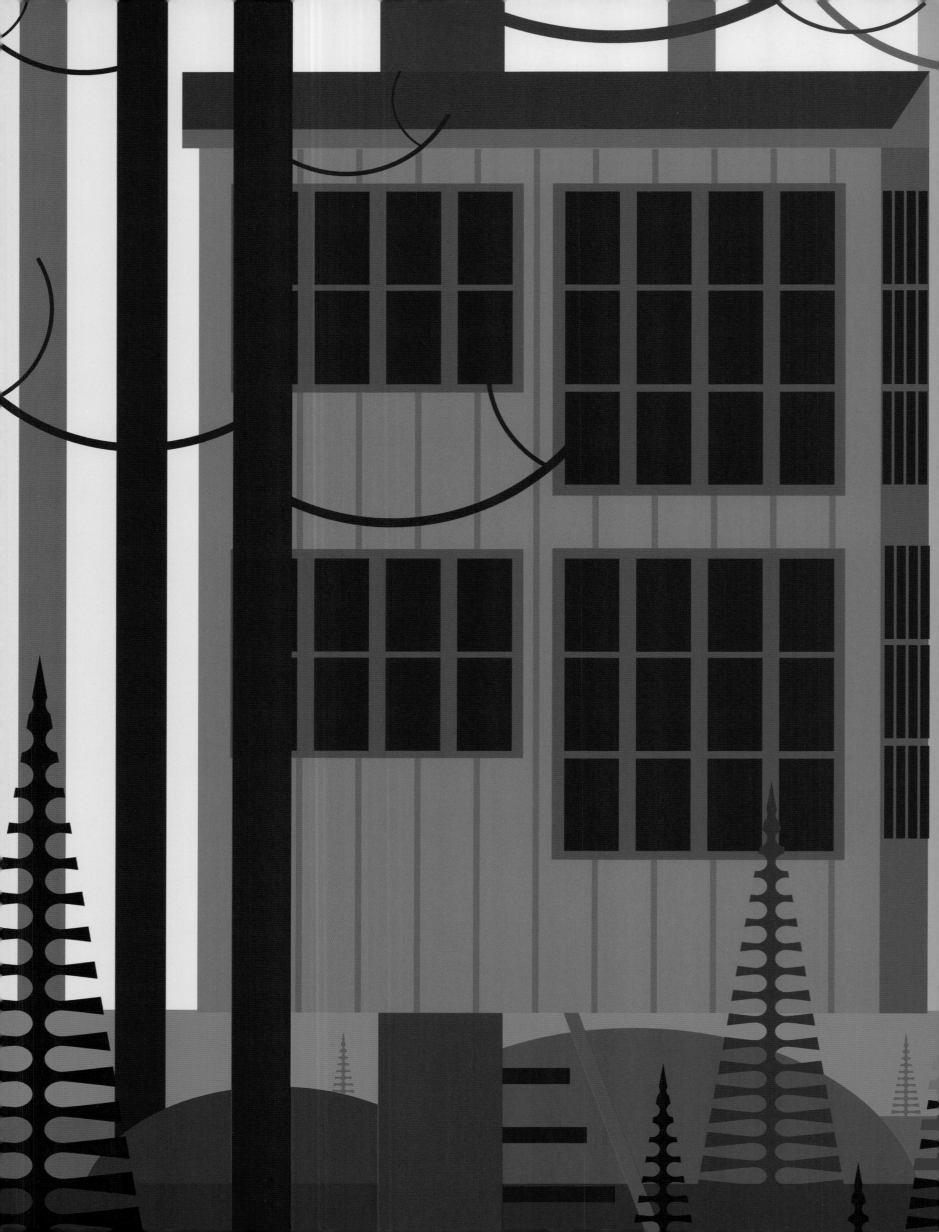

47

Designed by Pete Nelson
Fall City, Washington (USA)

trillium
tree house

Rather than being centered on a tree, this structure hangs from one side of a large western red cedar tree. The floor plan measures roughly 2.4 x 4.8 meters. It has a second-story loft that occupies half of this area, including a queen-size bed and an electric toilet. A closet, reading chairs, bookshelves, and a kitchen are located on the main level. The whole has a floor area of about 18.5 square meters. The tree house is reached via a spiral staircase that is wrapped around the tree, crossing over a pond on the way up.

Statt mittig um einen Baum gebaut zu sein, hängt dieses Baumhaus seitlich an einem Riesen-Lebensbaum. Sein Grundriss misst etwa 2,4 x 4,8 m. Das Mezzaningeschoss nimmt rund die Hälfte dieser Grundfläche in Anspruch: Hier befinden sich ein Doppelbett und eine elektrische Toilette. Auf der Hauptebene sind ein Wandschrank, Lesesessel, Bücherregale und eine Küche untergebracht. Die Nutzfläche beträgt ingesamt rund 18,5 m². Erschlossen wird das Baumhaus über eine Wendeltreppe, die sich um den Baum windet und auf dem Weg nach oben über einen Teich führt.

Cette maison n'est pas centrée sur un arbre mais suspendue au côté d'un grand cèdre rouge. Elle mesure 2,4 x 4,8 m au sol, mais possède un étage de la moitié de cette surface et comprend un lit de grandes dimensions et des toilettes électriques. Au niveau principal se trouvent des fauteuils, une kitchenette, une bibliothèque et un placard. La maison est accessible par un escalier en spirale autour du tronc de l'arbre qui franchit une mare au passage.

With its generous glazing and unusual form, the Trillium Tree House might be considered more contemporary than some other designs by Pete Nelson, but it retains his trademark spectacular appearance.

Durch die großzügige Verglasung und seine ungewöhnliche Form wirkt das Trillium Tree House vielleicht zeitgenössischer als andere Entwürfe von Pete Nelson, dennoch ist das Design typisch spektakulär.

Généreusement vitrée et de forme inhabituelle, la Trillium Tree House paraît sans doute plus contemporaine que d'autres projets de Pete Nelson, mais garde un aspect particulier qui lui est personnel.

The upper-level loft (bottom) covers only half the area of the plan, allowing for this stunning open space above the living area. The whole appears much larger than its 18 square-meter floor area.

Das Mezzaningeschoss (unten) nimmt rund die Hälfte der Grundfläche ein, wodurch über dem Wohnbereich eine beeindruckende Deckenhöhe entsteht. Der Raum wirkt wesentlich größer als seine 18 m² Grundfläche.

Le niveau supérieur ne représente que la moitié de la surface de la partie inférieure (ci-dessous), ce qui permet de créer un volume étonnant au-dessus du séjour. L'ensemble semble plus grand que ses 18 m².

48

Designed by Inredningsgruppen
Harads (Sweden) — 2008

ufo tree hotel

Part of the Harads Tree Hotel located in northern Sweden, the UFO is made of light, durable composite materials. It is intended for use by two adults and two children, with bedrooms (one with a double bed, the other with two single beds), bathroom, and a shared living space. The floor area of the interior is 30 square meters. The structure has a circular plan and there are two interior levels. Despite the unexpected reference to a UFO, this object, hanging in the trees, with its thin entrance stair seems very much like the sort of thing one could discover in the midst of a northern forest.

Das UFO-Baumhaus gehört zum Tree-Hotel-Komplex in Harads, Nordschweden, und wurde aus leichten, wetterbeständigen Verbundmaterialien gebaut. Es bietet Platz für zwei Erwachsene und zwei Kinder und hat zwei Schlafzimmer (eins mit Doppelbett, eins mit Einzelbetten), ein Bad sowie einen gemeinschaftlichen Wohnbereich. Die Nutzfläche beträgt 30 m². Der Bau mit rundem Grundriss hat zwei Ebenen. Trotz der ungewöhnlichen UFO-Thematik wirkt das in den Bäumen hängende Objekt mit seiner filigranen Zugangsleiter durchaus wie etwas, das man in einem Wald im Norden entdecken könnte.

Faisant partie du Harads Tree Hotel situé dans le nord de la Suède, l'UFO est en matériaux composites légers et durables. Prévu pour deux adultes et deux enfants, il comprend deux chambres (une avec lit double, l'autre deux lits simples), une salle de bains et un séjour. La surface intérieure est de 30 m² pour les deux niveaux de plan circulaire. Dans une sombre forêt nordique où tout peut arriver, la référence à un OVNI (UFO) semble naturelle pour cet objet suspendu dans les arbres et son échelle d'accès arachnéenne.

Designed by Gertil Harström, like the Bird's Nest Tree Hotel also published in this volume (p. 70), the UFO shares a circular plan with its counterpart but not much else—this UFO looks almost real!

Wie das Bird's Nest Hotel in diesem Band (S. 70) stammt auch dieser Entwurf von Gertil Harström. Abgesehen vom ebenfalls runden Grund-riss hat es kaum etwas mit seinem Pendant gemeinsam – das UFO wirkt fast echt!

Conçu par Gertil Harström, comme le Bird's Nest Tree Hotel présenté à la page 70), l'UFO est également de plan circulaire. On dirait un véritable OVNI !

49

Designed by Andreas Wenning (baumraum)
Eberschwang (Austria) — 2008

wagtail tree house

This project is located in a rural area between the cities of Salzburg and Linz. With a terrace suspended between a birch and two ash trees, the structure itself, connected by a catwalk, is supported on eight asymmetrically placed, leaning oak stilts. The terrace is 3.5 meters off the ground, while the actual tree house is a little over a meter higher. The owners wanted to be able to see their house from the tree structure, but also to be able to catch trout in a nearby stream from the terrace. They were not adverse to some architectural experimentation, which led Andreas Wenning to employ Corten steel. Untreated oak was used inside the 8.8-square-meter tree house. A panoramic window provides the requested view, while an integrated sound system allows the owners to listen to music in their tree house.

Das Projekt liegt in einer ländlichen Gegend zwischen Salzburg und Linz. Die Terrasse ist zwischen einer Birke und zwei Eschen aufgehängt, das über einen Steg erreichbare Baumhaus ruht auf acht asymmetrisch angeordneten, schrägen Eichenstützen. Während die Terrasse 3,5 m über dem Boden schwebt, liegt das eigentliche Baumhaus gut 1 m höher. Die Bauherren wollten einerseits ihr Wohnhaus sehen, andererseits von der Terrasse aus Forellen im nahen Bach angeln können. Offen für architektonische Experimente, ließen sie Andreas Wenning hier mit Cortenstahl arbeiten. Im Innern der 8,8 m² großen Kabine wurde unbehandelte Eiche verbaut; ein Panoramafenster bietet den gewünschten Ausblick.

Cette maison se trouve dans la campagne, entre Salzbourg et Linz. La structure reliée par une passerelle à une terrasse suspendue entre un bouleau et deux frênes repose sur huit piliers de chêne inclinés et disposés de façon asymétrique. La terrasse est à 3,5 m au-dessus du sol et la maison elle-même un mètre plus haut environ. Les propriétaires souhaitaient voir leur « vraie » maison de celle-ci, mais aussi pouvoir attraper les truites du ruisseau qui court non loin de la terrasse. Ils n'étaient pas opposés à une certaine expérimentation architecturale, ce qui a permis Andreas Wenning d'utiliser de l'acier Corten. L'intérieur de 8,8 m² est en chêne non traité. Une baie panoramique offre la vue demandée tandis qu'un système de sonorisation permet aux propriétaires d'écouter leur musique favorite.

This stunning structure is set up on tilted wooden columns that look like legs. It is approached via the steps and intermediate platform seen below, and to the left of the right page.

Die schrägen Holzstützen, auf denen der beeindruckende Bau ruht, erinnern an Beine. Der Zugang erfolgt über Treppen und eine Zwischen-plattform, unten und rechts im Bild.

Cette étonnante construction repose sur des colonnes de bois inclinées qui font penser à des jambes. On y accède par une échelle et une plate-forme intermédiaire (ci-dessous et page de droite).

The interior is almost fully glazed, even above, with a long skylight. Visitors can sleep here, or lie and look at the trees and sky. A real getaway!

Der Innenraum ist rundum verglast, sogar an der Decke gibt es ein langes Oberlicht. Gäste können hier schlafen oder im Liegen in die Bäume und den Himmel schauen. Ein wahrer Zufluchtsort!

L'intérieur est presque entièrement vitré, y compris une verrière oblongue. Les visiteurs peuvent y dormir, s'y étendre et regarder les arbres et le ciel. Un pur plaisir !

Designed by Peter Eising, Pacific Environments
Warkworth (New Zealand) — 2008

yellow tree house restaurant

This 44-square-meter tree-house restaurant was built for a cost of €320 000. The concept of this structure was to find all of the products and services required through Yellow Pages listings. A 40-meter-high redwood tree, 1.7 meters in diameter at its base, located north of Auckland, was selected for the project. Their design "has loose similarities to a seashell with the open ends spiraling to the center. It's the tree house we all dreamed of as children but could only do as an adult fantasy." The access to the restaurant is through a 60-meter treetop walkway. Despite its unexpected location, the restaurant seats 18 people and staff, and includes a bar. Kitchen and toilet facilities are located at ground level.

Die Baukosten des 44 m² großen Baumhausrestaurants beliefen sich auf 320 000 €. Konzeptvorgabe für diesen Bau war, alle benötigten Produkte und Dienstleistungen über die Gelben Seiten zu finden. Die Wahl für den Standort fiel auf einen 40 m hohen Mammutbaum nördlich von Auckland, mit einem Durchmesser von 1,7 m am Fuß des Baumes. Der Entwurf „erinnert im weitesten Sinne an eine Muschel, die sich von außen schneckenförmig nach innen schraubt. Es ist genau das Baumhaus, von dem wir als Kinder geträumt haben, eine Fantasie, die wir erst als Erwachsene realisieren konnten." Erschlossen wird das Restaurant über einen 60 m langen Steg zwischen den Bäumen. Trotz der ungewöhnlichen Lage bietet das Restaurant, zu dem auch eine Bar gehört, Platz für 18 Gäste und Servicepersonal. Küche und Toiletten liegen ebenerdig.

Ce restaurant dans un arbre de 44 m² a été construit pour un budget de 320 000 €. Le concept était de trouver tous les produits et services nécessaires au projet dans les Pages jaunes. Un séquoia de 40 m de haut et de 1,7 m de diamètre à sa base a été choisi non loin d'Auckland. Le projet « présente quelques similarités avec un coquillage dont la partie ouverte partirait en spirale vers l'intérieur. C'est la maison dans un arbre dont tout enfant a toujours rêvé mais qui ne peut se concrétiser qu'à l'âge adulte. » L'accès au restaurant se fait par une passerelle de 60 m de long. Malgré cette situation étonnante, le restaurant et son bar peuvent recevoir simultanément 18 convives et membres du personnel. La cuisine et les toilettes sont au sol.

The open structure of the restaurant seen here at night from its approach ramp. Glowing from within, the design retains a certain "natural" appearance although it is certainly modern as well.

Ein nächtlicher Blick über den Zugangssteg auf die offene Konstruktion des Restaurants. Der von innen leuchtende Bau ist von einer gewissen „Natürlichkeit", obwohl er zweifellos auch sehr modern ist.

La structure ouverte du restaurant vue de nuit, depuis sa rampe d'accès. L'architecture conserve une certaine apparence « naturelle » même si elle est résolument contemporaine.

A daylight view (left) emphasizes the "seashell" appearance of the architectural design. The approach ramp is at the rear of the picture on the left. Above, the dining space, and right, the splayed structure at the top of the restaurant.

Eine Ansicht bei Tageslicht (links) unterstreicht die Ähnlichkeit des Entwurfs mit einer Seemuschel. Der Zugangssteg ist links im Hintergrund zu sehen. Oben der Gastraum und rechts die Fächerkonstruktion an der Spitze des Restaurants.

Une vue diurne (à gauche) fait ressortir l'aspect « coquillage » du projet. La rampe d'accès est à l'arrière. Ci-dessus, la salle à manger et à droite, la « charpente » du restaurant.

tree-house designers

BAUMRAUM

Andreas Wenning
Borchersweg 14
28203 Bremen
Germany

Tel: +49 421 70 51 22
Fax: +49 42 17 94 63 51
E-mail: a.wenning@baumraum.de
Web: www.baumraum.de

Andreas Wenning was born in 1965. He studied as a cabinetmaker in Weinheim, Germany (1982–85), and as an architect at the Technical University of Bremen, where he obtained his degree in 1995. He worked in the office of José Garcia Negette in Sydney, Australia (2000–01), and he created his own office, baumraum, in Bremen in 2003. Aside from the tree houses published here, he has worked on weblike "grabnet" rope structures for trees (Lower Saxony Horticultural Show, Wolfsburg, 2004), and organized seminars on "The Body Language of Trees," and "Building a Tree House without Impairing the Tree." His firm offers to build unique tree houses for clients. In 2009 he published a book on his work entitled Baumhauser, Neue Architektur in den Bäumen *(Berlin).*

HORACE BURGESS

P.O. Box 1165
Crossville, TN 38557
USA

Tel: +1 931 265 3988

Horace Burgess is a full-time landscape designer and an ordained Christian minister. His tree house, published here, is also called the Minister's Tree House because of his principal occupation. He was self-taught as a carpenter as the ad hoc nature of the design of this structure implies. It does have a bell tower and has been used as a church. It is located on Beehive Lane in Crossville, Tennessee, which is a town with a population of 10 7895 people (2010 census). Crossville is the county seat of Cumberland County, Tennessee. The Minister's Tree House is technically not open to the public, but it is, nonetheless, visited by thousands of people who climb its 10 stories at their own risk.

CASA NA ÁRVORE

Lodrina, Paraná
Brazil

Tel: +55 43 3323 8858
E-mail: brunelli@casanaarvore.com
Web: www.casanaarvore.com

Casa na Árvore (meaning "house in a tree") is a tree-house construction company located in the south of Brazil, near the Argentine border. The company is run by Ricardo Brunelli on the business side and José Aparecido Rossato for the carpentry. They work with the engineer Everaldo Pletz. They started designing and building tree houses in 2001. Their first venture was an 84-square-meter tree house they built 10 meters off the ground around a 100-year-old fig tree on a farm in southern Brazil. Since then, they have built

numerous remarkable tree houses in the areas of Rio de Janeiro, São Paulo, and Paraná. They have also designed and built a number of playgrounds or facilities specifically meant for children.

MÅRTEN & GUSTAV CYRÉN

Mårten Cyrén Design
Banvägen 7
131 41 Nacka
Sweden

Tel: +46 8 55 61 57 55
E-mail: marten@cyren.se
Web: www.cyren.se

Mårten Cyrén was born in Upsala, Sweden, in 1958. He studied interior architecture and furniture design before founding Cyrén & Cyrén with his brother Gustav in 1997. His main firm today remains Mårten Cyrén Design in Nacka. His work has been mostly in the area of furniture design—with the Cabin at the Tree House Hotel in Harads, Sweden (published here), being one notable exception. His design work includes the tables for Pyra (2000), and the Vox lounge chair with an integrated sound system (Ire Möble, with Bertil Harström, 2010). He has worked for numerous Swedish firms including Ikea.

DANS MON ARBRE

Espace Vaucanson
82 Rue Anatole France
38100 Grenoble
France

Tel: +33 476 49 83 45
E-mail: dansmonarbre.sarl@gmail.com
Web: www.dansmonarbre.com

Renaud Morel
2 Impasse du Carré
69380 Les Chères
France

Tel: +33 607 65 35 73
E-mail: contact@renaudmorel-design.com

Benoît Fray
E-mail: benoit.fray@gmail.com
Profile of the architect:
http://www.coroflot.com/fray/profile

Frank Coursier is the founder of Dans mon Arbre. He continues to be directly involved in the technical and financial aspects of their projects. Some of the tree houses published here have been developed with Renaud Morel and Benoît Fray. The designers state: "Any human intervention in a tree is a source of different types of stress for the tree. Our profession is to limit that stress as much as possible. We run a diagnosis of any tree we plan to build in. Our tree houses are respectful of their hosts—the size and the height of the structures are calculated to correspond to the trees concerned; the systems we use to attach structural elements are designed to allow the free circulation of tree sap and thus to project the trees themselves." The design and construction of one of their typical projects takes between three months and one year and costs can be in the range of €2000 per square meter for an insulated tree house with water and electricity. The structures come with a

10-year guarantee. As French tree-house construction requires the same sort of building permit as any earth-bound architecture, Dans mon Arbre operates like many "normal" design-and-build companies.

NICKO BJORN ELLIOT

Matthew Baird Architects
325 Hudson Street, 9th floor
New York, NY 10013
USA

E-mail: nicko.elliott@gmail.com
Web: www.bairdarchitects.com

Nicko Elliot was born in Canada in 1980. He received his M.Arch degree from the University of Toronto (2005–09). He worked with Saucier Perrote Architectes in Montreal (2010–11) and was a lead designer in Bureau E.A.S.T. in Fez, Morocco, when they won the 2009 Global Holcim Awards Gold Award for Sustainable Construction for a project concerning the Fez river. He has been a project architect at Matthew Baird Architects in New York since 2011, but the tree house published here was realized as a personal project.

FREE SPIRIT SPHERES

420 Horne Lake Road
Qualicum Beach
British Columbia V9K 1 Z7
Canada

Tel: +1 250 757 9445
E-mail: tom@freespiritspheres.com
Web: www.freespiritspheres.com

Tom Chudleigh is the "inventor, manufacturer, and distributor" of Free Spirit Spheres. As he explains the creation: "The 'Spherical Tree House' concept borrows heavily from sailboat construction and rigging practice. It's a marriage of tree house and sailboat technology. Wooden spheres are built much like a cedar-strip canoe or kayak. Suspension points are similar to the chain plate attachments on a sailboat. Stairways hang from a tree much like a sailboat shroud hangs from the mast." From the current total of three spheres that can be rented—named Eve, Eryn, and Melody—Chudleigh hopes to eventually build more. These are located on two hectares of private forestland surrounding a pond near Qualicum Bay, Vancouver Island, British Columbia in Canada. "My personal goal is to produce 10 to 15 spheres and hang them all in a large area of old growth forest: a spiritual retreat for me and whoever else is interested," says Tom Chudleigh.

TERUNOBU FUJIMORI

Professor, Institute of Industrial Science
The University of Tokyo
4–6–1 Komaba, Meguro-ku
Tokyo 153–8505
Japan

Tel: +81 3 5452 6370
Fax: +81 3 5452 6371
E-mail: tanpopo@iis.u-tokyo.ac.jp

Born in Chino City, Nagano (Japan), in 1946, Terunobu Fujimori attended Tohoku University (1965–71) in Sendai before receiving his Ph.D. in Architecture from the University of Tokyo (1971–78). He is currently a professor at the University of Tokyo's Institute of Industrial Science. Although research on often long-forgotten Western-style buildings in Japan from the Meiji period onwards remains his main activity, he is also a practicing architect. "I didn't start designing buildings until my forties, so the condition I set for myself is that I shouldn't just repeat the same things that my colleagues or professors were doing," he has stated. His completed projects, aside from the three tree houses published here, include the Akino Fuku Art Museum (Hamamatsu, Shizuoka, 1995–97); Nira House (Leek House, Machida City, Tokyo 1995–97); Student Dormitory for Kumamoto Agricultural College (Koshi City, Kumamoto, 1998–2000); and the Ichiya-tei (One Night Tea House, Ashigarashimo, Kanagawa, 2003). He recently participated in the Sumika Project (Coal House, Utsunomiya, Tochigi, 2008) with Toyo Ito and other well-known architects, and completed the Copper House (Kokubunji City, Tokyo, 2009), all in Japan.

HAPUKU LODGE

State Highway 1 at Station Road, RD 1
Kaikoura
South Island
New Zealand

Tel: +64 3 319 6559
Fax: +64 3 319 6557
E-mail: info@hapukulodge.com
Web: www.hapukulodge.com/kaikoura

Hapuku Lodge is run by Tony Wilson, whose father was the New Zealand Government Architect from 1949 to 1959. Tony Wilson studied history and then law at UCLA. He created Wilson Associates with his two younger brothers, both architects, and their sister Sara in 1982 to "design, build, and operate small, high-quality, real-estate properties." They also created a number of restaurants. In New Zealand, Tony Wilson created the Hapuku Deer Farm with a nephew in the early 1990s. Wilson Associates then built a guest house on this property. The team has designed the more recent tree houses and other structures, as well as their furnishings. They have taken a keen interest in the ecological responsibility of their work. Condé Nast Traveler magazine selected Hapuku Lodge as one of the "best hotels for honeymoons."

GO HASEGAWA

Go Hasegawa & Associates
2–18–7 Gaien Building 5F,
Jingumae, Shibuya-ku
Tokyo 150–0001
Japan

Tel: +81 3 3403 0336
Fax: +81 3 3403 0337
E-mail: office@hsgwg.com
Web: www.hsgwg.com

Go Hasegawa was born in 1977 in Saitama, Japan. He completed a Master's degree at the Tokyo Institute of Technology, Graduate School of Science and Engineering (2002), before working in the office of Taira Nishizawa (2002–04). He founded Go Hasegawa & Associates in 2005. His work includes the House in a Forest (Nagano, 2006); House in Sakuradai (Mie, 2006); House in Gotanda (Tokyo, 2006); House in Komae (Tokyo, 2009); Nerima Apartment (Tokyo, 2010); and Pilotis in a Forest (Gunma, 2010, published here).

MICHAEL INCE

61A Burnett Lane
Brookhaven, NY 11719
USA

Tel: +1 631 286 5870

Michael Ince is an artist and boat builder. He creates works of art and environments based in part on the wildlife and imagery of the marshes of Long Island. He creates abstract sculptures, drawings, prints, and objects often inspired by birds. He has also designed benches made of wood and stone, for example. Using recycled wood, he has also built tree houses for children, or architectural follies. He grew up in Brookhaven (Long Island), New York, and graduated from Bowdoin College in Maine in 1964. As well as the tree house published here, another significant tree house he designed is the Marsh House, which is on the grounds of his Long Island home.

INKATERRA

Andalucia 174, Miraflores
Lima 18
Peru

Tel: +51 1 610 0400
Fax: +51 1 422 4701
E-mail: claire.andre@inkaterra.com
Web: www.inkaterra.com

Inkaterra has been involved in ecotourism since 1975. They describe themselves as "a 100% carbon neutral and exclusive Peruvian tourism organization and boutique hotel developer dedicated to conserving the country's natural and cultural heritage through various social projects." Inkaterra was finalist in the World Travel and Tourism Council Conservation Award 2010, granted in Beijing. The WTTC description of Inkaterra reads: "Through its hotel operations, as well as established ecotourism products, such as the Inkaterra Canopy Walk or the Anaconda Walk, Inkaterra funds its extensive research projects, the results of which have been published in numerous prestigious publications, and have led to the discovery of 15 new-to-science species on its premises. Inkaterra is also a leader in environmental conservation, documenting Peruvian traditional culture on DVD and CD recordings. The company employs 500 people, many of them members of the local community; it hosts a great number of visiting researchers at its own cost and welcomes 46000 guests annually."

INREDNINGSGRUPPEN

Tunbyn 202
855 90 Sundsval
Sweden

Tel: +46 60 12 1655
E-mail: bertil@inredningsgruppen
Web: www.inredningsgruppen.se

Bertil Harström was born in 1948. He studied at the Industrial Art School (Konstindustriskolan) of Göteborg (1977–81). He worked in the office of White Arkitekter (Göteborg, 1981–85) before founding Inredningsgruppen (Interior

Group) in 1987. He is the owner and managing director of the firm. He is essentially a product designer, having created numerous objects for Glimakra. He has won three Swedish Design Awards. He was project leader for VISTET (1997–99), the first FSC-certified European house made of wood (architects Anders Landström and Thomas Sandell). He has also designed objects with Mårten Cyrén such as the Luna "Sound Seat," a chair with an integrated audio system for Lammhuits Library Design.

TAKASHI KOBAYASHI

Treehouse Creations Co., Ltd.

Tel/Fax: +81 3 5410 2343
E-mail: info@treehouse.jp
Web: www.treehouse.jp/thp_eng/koba.html

Treehouse Creations was incorporated in Tokyo in 2005 by Takashi Kobayashi. It is part of the non-profit Japan Tree House Network. "As a company," says Kobayashi, "it is dedicated to guiding people in the proper design, construction, and maintenance of completed tree houses, as well as management of the grounds where they stand." Kobayashi dates his own interest in tree houses to a moment 17 years ago when he discovered a Himalaya cedar growing in an alleyway in Tokyo's Harajuku district. He now says that he will continue to be involved in this profession "as long as there are undiscovered trees still waiting…" The Hideaway Café is now built around this cedar in Harajuku and contains a library of tree-house related books, souvenirs, and information: see <www.treehouse.jp/hideaway>.

LUKASZ KOS

four o nine
90 Yuqing Lu, 2–302
Shanghai 200030
China

Tel: +86 186 0178 7594
E-mail: info@four-o-nine.com
Web: www.four-o-nine.com

Lukasz Kos was born in Starachowice, Poland, in 1978. He studied environmental design at the University of Manitoba (Canada, 2000), and obtained an M.A. degree from the Jagiellonian University, Center for European Studies (Cracow, 2003). He received his M.Arch from the University of Toronto, Faculty of Architecture Landscape and Design (Canada, 2006). He has worked recently for Maclennan Jaunkalns Miller Architects (Toronto, Canada, 2009–10) and for Bruce Mau Design (Toronto). He has also worked as an Adjunct Assistant Professor at the University of Toronto, Daniels Faculty of Architecture Landscape and Design (2009–10).

LES NIDS

Montpugin 8
2400 Le Locle
Switzerland

Tel: +41 32 931 32 59 / Fax: +41 32 931 32 50
E-mail: info@lesnids.ch
Web: www.lesnids.ch

Located in the canton of Neuchâtel (Switzerland), Le Locle is a town of about 12 000 inhabitants located at an altitude of 1000 meters above sea level. The area is ideal for tourism, football, mini-golf, or such sports as cross-country skiing in winter. The Nids (nests) published here are tree houses built in healthy ash trees between five and eight meters above the ground. The facility is run by Jean-Paul and Karin Vuilleumier.

LION SANDS

Sabi Sand Game Reserve
Mpumalanga
South Africa

Tel/Fax: +27 13 735 5000/5330
E-mail: gabyr@lionsands.com
Web: www.lionsands.com

The private game reserve at Lion Sands was founded in 1933 when Guy Aubrey Chalkley purchased the land from the Transvaal Consolidated Mines company. It is now owned by fourth-generation descendants of Chalkley, the More family. Lion Sands is located in the territory of the Sabi Sand Game Reserve, Mpumalanga, South Africa. Forming part of the greater Kruger National Park, the reserve has no fences and the wildlife is able to cross freely between Lion Sands and the Kruger National Park.

NELSON TREEHOUSE AND SUPPLY

PO Box 1135
Fall City, WA 98024
USA

Tel: +1 425 441 8568
E-mail: info@nelsontreehouseandsupply.com
Web: www.nelsontreehouseandsupply.com

Pete Nelson, the owner of Nelson TreeHouse and Supply Llc, is one of the best-known authors on the subject. His firm has built "unique tree houses" all across the United States. They also offer workshops and consulting services for those who prefer to build their own tree house. Pete Nelson was born in Mineola, New York, in 1962. Though he built tree houses as a child with his father, it was the discovery of a book sent to him by a friend on how to build tree houses that convinced Nelson of his vocation. His own 1994 book, Treehouses, the Art and Craft of Living Out On a Limb, *represents a first publishing effort that met with success. In 1997 he created the TreeHouse Workshop with Jake Jacob, before setting up his present firm. Aside from books including* Treehouses of the World *(New York, 2004), Pete Nelson has also worked recently on the Northwest Treehouse School, a teaching facility for design and construction; Treehouse Point, an "environmental tree house retreat center;" and the Tree for All Foundation, "a non-profit corporation inspired by the work of Bill Allen of Forever Young that brings disabled people into nature and tree houses."*

O2 TREEHOUSE

15102 Balso Chica Suite F
Huntington Beach, CA 92645
USA

120 North 4th Street
Minneapolis, MN 56623
USA

Tel: +1 612 636 6656
E-mail: info@o2treehouse.com
Web: www.02treehouse.com

Built with sustainable materials, O2 tree houses are based in their design on the geodesic dome originally created by Buckminster Fuller. One of the main features of the geodesic dome is that it allows construction with the minimum amount of materials for a given volume. The modular system developed by Dustin Feider, a 23-year-old freelance furniture designer from Minneapolis, allows for a great variety of different types of solutions based on this simple form. Dustin Feider graduated from the Minneapolis College of Art and Design in Furniture Design. He worked for a year and a half at Brandow Creative, an interior design studio in Minneapolis, before beginning to develop the O2 Sustainability Tree House. The mounting system for the O2 tree house allows for unrestricted tree growth. Making use of translucent 0.16-centimeter-thick polypropylene panels, the O2 tree houses can appear to glow from within at night. The price of these tree houses begins at about $6800 and up.

SEAN ORLANDO AND FIVE TON CRANE

Tel: +1 415 515 1239
E-mail: seano@engineeredartworks.com
Web: www.engineeredartworks.com / www.fivetoncrane.org/blog/

The Steampunk Tree House is presently located at the:
Dogfish Head Craft Brewery
#6 Cannery Village Center
Milton, DE 19968
USA

Tel: +1 302 684 1000
Web: www.dogfish.com

Sean Orlando is a cofounder of the Oakland-based Five Ton Crane Arts Group, a founding member of Kinetic Steam Works, and one of the lead artists on the Raygun Gothic Rocketship project, a site-specific group sculpture project created for the Burning Man event in 2009. He was the "lead artist / designer of the Steampunk Tree House, a site-specific group sculpture project created for the Burning Man event in 2007."

Five Ton Crane (5TC) is a group of "artists, geeks, and inventors" from the San Francisco Bay Area. As they describe their own work: "5TC does the heavy lifting that the individual artist couldn't do on his own; by pooling resources, interests, and talent to create opportunities for bigger, better, and bolder Art."

PACIFIC ENVIRONMENTS

Pacific Environments NZ Ltd Architects
81 Grafton Road Level 4
Auckland
New Zealand

Tel: +64 09 308 0070
Fax: +64 09 308 0071
E-mail: info@pacificenvironments.co.nz
Web: www.pacificenvironments.co.nz

Born in 1959 in Wellington, New Zealand, Peter Eising obtained his B.Arch degree from the University of Auckland in 1984. From 1977 to 1984 he worked as a draftsman in the Ministry of Works and Development in Wellington. In 1988, he set up Architects Patterson Limited with Andrew Patterson. He was a Director of that firm until 2006, when he became the Director of Pacific Environments. Lucy Gauntlett was born in 1981 in Melbourne, Australia. She graduated from the School of Architecture at Auckland University in 2004. She is also a professional photographer. As well as the Tree House Restaurant published here, their work includes the Crater Lake House (Orakei, Auckland, 2004–06); the Laidlaw Commercial Business Park (East Tamaki, Auckland, 2005–06); Tristar Gymnasium (Mt. Roskill, Auckland, 2004–07); and St. Stephens Avenue Apartments (Parnell, Auckland, 2006–07). Their current work includes Navy Training Facilities (Shakespear's Point, Whangaparaoa Peninsula, 2005–); and the Oceanic Artifacts Museum (Bora Bora, Tahiti, French Polynesia, 2008–), all in New Zealand.

PEZULU TREE HOUSE GAME LODGE

PO Box 795
Hoedspruit, 1380
Limpopo Province
South Africa

Tel: +27 15 793 2724
Fax: +27 15 793 2253
E-mail: pezlodge@mweb.co.za
Web: www.pezulu.co.za

Pezulu is situated in the Guernsey Private Nature Reserve in the Limpopo province of South Africa, 40 minutes from Kruger National Park. The Lodge is made up of seven thatch and reed tree houses, accommodating a maximum of 16 people. Each unit "has been built to blend with the environment whilst maintaining an element of luxury." No nails penetrate the trees; rather, the all-wood structures have been built around the trees, allowing large, live branches to pass through the tree houses. The Pezulu tree houses also have an outdoor shower or bath, running hot water, electricity, and... mosquito nets. They are located at a sufficient distance from each other to provide for complete privacy.

RODERICK WOLGAMOTT ROMERO

Romero Studios
169 Avenue A, Apt 5A
New York, NY 10009
USA

Tel: +1 646 295 4325
E-mail: romerostudios@gmail.com
Web: www.romerostudios.com

Roderick Wolgamott Romero was born in 1965 in Seattle, Washington. He attended the University of Washington and studied medicine. He studied theater in Paris (École Jacques Lecoq), and recorded several albums with his group Sky Cries Mary. Romero Studios was created by Roderick and Anisa Romero in 1997. The purpose of the studio has always been the design and construction of sustainable or green tree houses. The couple has a background in painting, sculpture, and music, and their clients have included Sting and Trudie Styler, Julianne Moore, Van Kilmer, and Donna Karan. Since 2009, Anisa Romero has been working with her own firm, Anisa Romero Art & Design. Romero Studios seeks to use local craftsmen for each project, and above all insists that the great majority (98%) of the materials be reclaimed or salvaged.

SANDELLSANDBERG

Ostermalmsgatan 26A
11426 Stockholm
Sweden

Tel: +46 40 601 91 30
E-mail: info@sandellsandberg.se
Web: www.sandellsandberg.se

SandellSandberg was founded in 1995 by Thomas Sandell, Ulf Sandberg, and Joakim Uebel. The firm was divided in two in 2004. A new affiliate, Grow, a brand development company, was created at that time under the leadership of Joakim Uebel. The two firms continue to share the same premises and collaborate on concept development, corporate identity projects, product design, and retail environments. SandellSandberg has approximately 30 employees. As well as the tree hotel published here, their work includes Villa Nilsson (Oland, 2001); Villa Ahlström (Värmdö, 2008); Melbystrand (Melbystrand, 2010); and Parhus Kottla (Lindingö, 2010), all in Sweden.

SCHNEIDER+SCHUMACHER

Schneider+Schumacher Planungsgesellschaft mbH
Poststraße 20A
60329 Frankfurt am Main
Germany

Tel: +49 69 25 62 62 33 / Fax: +49 69 25 62 62 99
E-mail: office@schneider-schumacher.de
www.schneider-schumacher.de

Till Schneider was born in Koblenz in 1959. He studied at the Kaiserslautern University and TH Darmstardt (1979–86) and did postgraduate studies with Peter Cook at the Städelschule Frankfurt. He cofounded Schneider+Schumacher in Frankfurt in 1988. Michael Schumacher was born in 1959 in Krefeld. He also studied at the Kaiserslautern University (1978–85) and did postgraduate work with Peter Cook in Frankfurt (1986), before forming his partnership with Till Schneider. He worked one year in the office of Norman Foster (London, 1987). As well as the tree house published here, their work includes the Silvertower (Frankfurt, 2011); Städel Museum (Frankfurt, 2012); the Autobahn Church (Siegerland, 2012); and the FAIR Accelerator Facility (Darmstadt, 2018, under construction), all in Germany.

THAM & VIDEGÅRD ARKITEKTER

Tham & Videgård Arkitekter
Blekingdegatan 46
11662 Stockholm
Sweden

Tel: +46 8 702 00 46
Fax: +46 8 702 00 56
E-mail: info@tvark.se
Web: www.tvark.se

Tham & Videgård was created in 1999 in Stockholm, Sweden. It is still directed by its cofounders and chief architects Bolle Tham (born in 1970) and Martin Videgård (born in 1968). Tham & Videgård completed the Kalmar Museum of Art (Kalmar, Sweden, 2004–08), and the new Moderna Museet Malmö, the Swedish Museum of Modern Art that opened to the public in 2009. They are currently working on the New School of Architecture and the new Campus Entrance at the Royal Institute of Technology (Valhallavägen, Stockholm, 2007–); completion is planned for 2013. Tham & Videgård is recognized as one of the significant newer firms on the international architecture scene and their involvement in the Harads Tree House Hotel (published in this volume) is a clear indication of the rising interest in tree architecture.

TREE HOUSES OF HAWAII

PO Box 389
Hana
Hawaii, HI 96713
USA

Tel: +1 808 248 7241
E-mail: hanatreehouse@yahoo.com
Web: www.treehousesofhawaii.com

David Greenberg lives on the Island of Maui in Hawaii. He studied architecture and urban design and "tried to rebuild Los Angeles after the riots of the early 1990s," deciding instead to "escape to Hawaii to start a new life." Inspired by early 1970s hippie tree-house experiments he had seen on the island of Kauai while a student, he became interested in "creating an architecture that was in sympathy and connected to nature particularly in tropical climates." He has designed four tree houses in Hawaii and four in China. He is also involved in promoting the use of bamboo through INBAR, the International Network for Bamboo and Rattan. He calls himself a "sustainable ruralist." David Greenberg is the author of a conceptual book called Tree Houses in Paradise (New York, 2006), and coauthor of Visionary Bamboo Designs for Ecological Living (Hawaii, 2007).

PHOTO CREDITS

All illustrations by Patrick Hruby © TASCHEN / **6–33** © Harald Melcher/Rubinland / **36–39** © Lukasz Kos / **42–45** © Benoît Fray/Dans mon Arbre / **46–49** © Pete Nelson / **52–57** © Alaisdair Jardine / **60–63** © Pete Nelson / **66, 68** © David Greenberg, Tree Houses of Hawaii / **67, 69** © Pete Nelson / **72–75** Inredningsgruppen © Treehotel / **78, 80–81** © Åke E:son Lindman / **79, 82–83** SandellSandberg © Treehotel / **86, 89** © Åke E:son Lindman / **87–88** Mårten & Gustav Cyrén © Treehotel / **92-95** © Inkaterra / **98–99** © Lion Sands / **102–107** © Jörg Hempel Photodesign / **110–113** © Michael Döring / **116–121** © Alaisdair Jardine / **124–127** © Pezulu Tree House Lodge / **130–133** © Pete Nelson / **136, 138 bottom** © Tom Chudleigh / **137, 139 top** © Denis Beauvais / **138 top, 139 bottom** © Jasper Bosman / **142–147** © Alaisdair Jardine / **150–153** © O2 / **156–159** © Emmanuelle Satti / **162–167** © Hapuku Lodge / **170–171** © Gilles Rozan/Dans mon Arbre / **174–177** © O2 / **180–183** © Pete Nelson / **186–189** © Terunobu Fujimori / **192–195** © baumraum Andreas Wenning / **198–201** © Renaud Morel/Dans mon Arbre / **204–209** Chris Yorke © Pete Nelson / **212–215** © Roderick Wolgamott Romero / **218–219** © ENÉA / **222–225** © Les Nids (Jean-Paul Vuilleumier) / **228–231** © Alaisdair Jardine / **234–237** © Nico Marziali / **240–241, 245 bottom, 246** © Åke E:son Lindman / **242–245 top, 247** Tham & Videgård Arkitekter © Treehotel / **250–253** © Jesse Colin Jackson / **256–259** © Markus Bollen / **262–265** © Alaisdair Jardine / **268–271** © Pete Nelson / **274–279** © Iwan Baan / **282–285** © Stepan Vrzala / **288–291** © Pete Nelson / **294–397** © Pete Nelson / **300–303** © Sean Orlando and the Five Ton Crane Arts Group / **306–309** © Terunobu Fujimori / **312–315** © Akihisa Masuda / **318–321** © Pete Nelson / **324–327** © Pete Nelson / **330–331** Inredningsgruppen © Treehotel / **334–337** © Alaisdair Jardine / **340–343** © Lucy Gauntlett

IMPRINT

Patrick Hruby grew up in a log cabin in the forests of Spirit Lake, Idaho. He later attended Art Center College of Design in Pasadena, Californa. He now works as an illustrator in Los Angeles.

Illustrations: **Patrick Hruby, Los Angeles**
Design: **Benjamin Wolbergs, Berlin**
Project Management: **Florian Kobler, Berlin**
Collaboration: **Harriet Graham, Turin**
and Inga Hallsson, Cologne
Production: **Ute Wachendorf and Tina**
Ciborowius, Cologne
German translation **Kristina Brigitta Köper, Berlin**
French translation: **Jacques Bosser, Montesquiou**
Printed in Germany

ISBN 978–3–8365–2664–7

© 2012 TASCHEN GmbH
Hohenzollernring 53
D–50672 Cologne

www.taschen.com